GUS

THE DOG FROM KENNEL G212

by Shawn Kendrick

I0164342

First published in Great Britain

Copyright © Shawn Kendrick 2020

Shawn Kendrick has asserted the moral right to be identified as the author of this work.

978-1-735-5216-1-9 (paperback)
978-1-735-5216-2-6 (hardback)

All rights reserved. No part of this publication may be reproduced, stored in a retrieval system, or transmitted, in any form or by any means, electronic, mechanical, photocopying, recording or otherwise, without the prior permission of the publisher.

"Two feet move the body.

Four paws move the soul."

- Shawn Murray Kendrick

Contents

Preface

MY LIFE HAD changed when I walked into the dog shelter, back on that January day in 2013. I went to inquire about volunteering. Instead, I left, heading to the pet store to pick up what I needed for my new friend. Things happen in our lives for a reason. It might take days, weeks, or even years, to understand why. For me, it took only minutes.

A little over two years ago, I lost Gus. Soon afterward, I began writing a journal of our life together as a therapy to help me cope with my loss. Eventually, I decided to turn it into a book to tell my story about Gus, my greatest gift in life, who is also my soulmate.

Regardless of the type of pet owner you are, I hope that you will see yourself within the pages of this book. And perhaps along your journey, my story brings you comfort, joy, and laughter, in remembrance of your pet.

1

5:47 P.M. JULY 6, 2018. A hazy evening. I don't quite remember what the weather was like outside. Inside my heart, a storm spun and had begun to knock the air out of my lungs.

A friend, a companion, a soul mate who had shown me the meaning of life, found me at my worst, and who, perhaps, loved me more than I loved myself, was dying. Gus was dying.

Letting go is painful, but it teaches you some of the most beautiful lessons in life. I can safely say that Gus had changed my life for the better. It was an unexpected friendship that was nothing less than a stroke of serendipity-the kind of friendship that changes you from the inside and makes you a better human being. But it wasn't a human or a person who did this to me. It was a dog.

2012 was quite a year for me. So much had happened in such a short amount of time. My marriage had ended on an awful note, and I, honestly, was shattered for quite a while. I was handling one of the most difficult and challenging structural steel construction projects of my career as a Project Manager. Life had become so overwhelming all of a sudden. And, with no one to offer me a shoulder to lean on, loneliness often crept in.

But hitting rock bottom is a telltale sign that your life's trajectory is only going to shoot up. And that's what was about to happen to me very, very soon.

I had two houses-a rental that was occupied by tenants and another, which I had shared with my now ex-wife. When we separated, we agreed that she would keep the new house and I would keep the rental.

I wasn't living in the house of my dreams, but I was more than grateful for the home. The friend I lived with ran a dog boarding business from his home. I often shared my bathroom with an aging, diabetic Shih Tzu. The little guy almost always peed on the floor, leaving a mess for me to clean up. But no complaints, because at least I had a dog to give me company.

Over time, I had grown accustomed to the furry pals around the house, wagging their tails in playfulness and love. Unknowingly, my heart began cultivating a special love for these dogs. I didn't mind sharing a 5 x 8 room with one. Large breed dogs, especially the boxer, were my favorites. There's something so special about boxers. They're tall, confident, and have an alluring luster that I could only aspire to have. Watching as my friend's life revolved around dogs, I could see how happy and reassured he felt. Reassurance-Love-Empathy.

My heart had been searching for all of these for such a long time. I had looked for this in human relationships, and I did receive my share of love. But this time around, the future seemed so bleak, uncertain, and terrifying. The only time I felt relieved from such worries was when I was busy with my construction project. In a way, I was thankful that my job kept me preoccupied during most of the day. It gave a structure and routine to my life that prevented me from succumbing to loneliness. If I wasn't working, I'd drink a beer or two. Think about life. Search for answers. It was during these moments when I wished so desperately that everything would return to the way it was.

With no family, no pets, no companion to share my thoughts with, I had increasingly become gloomy and sulky. Emotional episodes came without warning, and I had to suffer through them all quietly. I hate to say it, but life can even compel a man to pull the trigger. But God held me back every time.

But even when my thoughts were dark and desperate, for the most part, I often felt a silent, unexplainable force pushing my heart to reach out and seek love. Quietly and softly, the way snowflakes melt into the ground, my heart made room for a companion who was going to change my life forever.

In my previous house, we had a boxer named Bruno. He was quite a handsome dog, who I would like to have taken with me, but my living arrangements didn't allow for it. Leaving the house, its people—my wife and my lovely stepdaughter—was heart-wrenching. Even now, the memories overwhelm me. I moved out of my friend's house just before Christmas and back into the house that I had as a rental.

By this time, I had mostly given up on relationships. Not because I was disappointed but perhaps because my heart wanted someone more faithful and wholesome, someone who'd stick around with me for good.

I often thought of getting a dog often when I felt most lonely and abandoned. I knew with all my heart that the love of a canine surpasses every kind of love. I had always had a dog to take care of, feed, and play with, except now.

2

IT HAD BEEN 25 years since I lived alone. Could I get used to this silence? Could I get used to not getting up early before work and letting my dog out? Could I live without taking my dog for a walk or to the vet? Could I live a life like this? If yes, for how long?

The void ate away at my strength. I was losing. I've always been fond of dogs and loved taking care of them, but getting one during these crucial days of my life? I felt hesitant.

The questions and fears flustered me. Would I be able to rekindle my feelings for a pet again? Whenever I went out, my neighbors would nosily inquire, "Where is your wife?" "How is your daughter?" "Are they not living with you?"

And, each time, I had to make up an answer or distract them. Loneliness is hauntingly scary, especially when people always remind you about it. Each time that happened, I had to crumple my feelings into a ball, put them aside to deal with later, and collect myself to face the world again. But I didn't want to experience this alone. The one thought that didn't leave my side was whether I should get a dog or not.

The house I was living in was quite a lovely house. The lavish comfort was undeniable—brand-new hardwood floors, sleek tiles, new kitchen cabinets, new carpet, and a fresh coat of paint on the inside and out. But my house didn't feel like a home. The emptiness, the silence, the absence of laughter—all of it pierced my heart.

Unknowingly, these emotions were pushing me to the brink of a life-altering decision. I had decided I was either going to get a dog or volunteer at a dog shelter.

Frankly, my heart didn't have room for dating anymore. I'd always found it to be risky and undeniable at the same time. But the companionship of a dog? Oh boy, there's nothing like it. It's pure, unconditional, and life-giving. And that is all I wanted.

It was a decision that had been pending. But now that I was alone, looking after a dog meant double the responsibility. Who was going to look after it while I'd be away? Would a puppy be right or a large dog to keep me company? If I were to volunteer instead of adopting, would I be able to give 100 percent?

I plunged into an abyss of doubts. The answers were hazy or, perhaps, hadn't arrived at my door yet.

So I did what any man with an undying love for dogs would do—I headed to the animal shelter. Wishing for the emotional turbulence to settle, I sought some canine therapy.

Walking into the shelter took me back to a tender and memorable time when I was once a pet owner. The dogs were tired, hungry, and scared. Somehow—in an ironic sort of way—the winces, moans, and barks coming from the cages were like music to my ears.

It didn't matter if I were to adopt or volunteer, for all I wanted was to become one with a canine. My feet involuntarily led me to the building that housed the "lost and stray." Perhaps, I, too, felt similarly. I looked left and right at each beautiful but terrified dog. My heart wanted to embrace all of them at once. After I took a few more steps down that particular aisle, I met my everlasting friend.

At the far end of the building, perhaps where no visitor had gone, there was a cage. It was the last kennel in the room. The final stray dog of the shelter was going to be my charm. It was a beautiful male boxer sitting

on a slender pair of legs. His eyes were warm but tired. They suddenly became windows through which I caught a glimpse of his physical and emotional turmoil. His fawn coat was nothing short of beautiful.

In my heart, I knew this boxer had been through a lot. He was whimpering and had no name. But this canine stood out the most. With a distinct pinkish birthmark etched on his upper lip, I knew in my heart that this dog had a story to tell.

I ushered the beautiful boxer to come to me. Emaciated, worn out, and dirty, he walked decisively toward me as if we were meant for each other. All the worries, fears, and doubts dissipated. He leaned up against the cage and I caressed his body. I shook his paw and could see his willingness. We shared an affectionate glance and knew what was to follow. Somehow, both of us were waiting for an angel to save our souls. And we had found each other.

His gentle demeanor, inquisitiveness, and intelligence were unlike that of a typical lost and stray dog. He deserved my home. And I wanted his loving company. I made my way to the lobby to speak with the manager on duty. After 45 minutes or so, the manager told me to return the next day. They needed to schedule a time for the following day to put him through the two tests required to be adopted out: the food aggression test and the dog aggression test. I asked to be present for the tests, and they agreed.

I left in a great mood. I had no reservations at all about the dog passing the tests. The gentleness and genuine spirit I had experienced put my mind at ease and my heart in the right place.

The rest of the night, I pondered over how he approached me, his eagerness to fall into my arms, to be caressed, and loved. What was it in me that made him so gentle and kind? Was he like that with everyone he met? The connection was clear; we both had a wounded soul. He was a boxer, and I was a boxer lover.

The next day, I was a wreck. I returned to the facility again and waited patiently. That beautiful dog gracefully walked on a leash like he had been doing it his entire life. My face lit up the moment I saw him, and I kneeled to call him.

The boxer put his paws on my hands. His touch was soft and gentle. He wagged his tail in anticipation and love as he got closer. And then we broke into hugs and kisses. At that moment, I wished I was a dog myself to communicate and tell him to do well in the tests. There was no way I was ever going to let go of him.

The next 30 minutes were going to be intense, if not downright excruciating. They were going to make me or break me. As I stood there, silently watching the two men administer the first test, the food aggression test, my boy acted like a true gentleman. The minute they tried removing the food bowl, he backed away. The next test was to stick a fake hand in his face while he ate. Again, he passed with flying colors.

We had one more test to pass. That would be the dog aggression test. The two gentlemen walked him up and down aisle after aisle, waiting to see if he would respond negatively. Every time he walked by, without even a hint of aggression, my smile would get bigger.

The clock struck 12:43 p.m. The tests were over. Told to go back up to the lobby, I couldn't help but believe that I would be leaving with a new friend. I looked around, my eyes searching for someone…anyone to come out.

Suddenly, a shadowy figure appeared that looked like a man pulling at a leash from the building's corridor. Was there a dog with him? Why were they sauntering?

And so it happened. The manager had walked the dog out. The boxer came walking as gracefully as before. At that moment, I realized why God had stopped me every time I had contemplated pulling the trigger. It was this moment that I had been waiting for all along. God wished for me to savor the euphoric joy as the boxer leaped into my arms. He was going home with me, but I had to wait until the next day. The protocol called for neutering before going to his new home.

I drove back home and prepared for his arrival. The checklist was complete. I had everything I needed to look after this boy— a water bowl, a leash, collars, toys, kennel, food bowl. The only thing I had to pick was some high-quality dog food.

I enthusiastically changed my house for him. I was changing everything inside the house for the dog. He had successfully entered my life. But what I didn't know was how he would begin to change me.

That night, as I sat in my backyard, reflecting at how everything was starting to fall in place, I realized that my newfound companion didn't have a name. The boxers I had owned previously were given their names by my nieces. This time around, the task was on me.

As I readied my home, it hit me that I had brought back some paperwork. I took it out to have a good look at his profile. His innocent picture left me teary-eyed. I was feeling a myriad of emotions that I couldn't express. I was happy, thinking that my house won't feel empty anymore, that I'll have a new member to look after. His arrival was perfect. It was just when I needed someone.

But what about the broken, lost, and worn look on his face? Who was ever going to save him? My eyes welled with tears as I vowed to myself to always stick by his side and give him the best life. As I gazed at his endearing picture, a name popped into my head, as if it were meant just for him. Gus. It was short and sweet. So Gus it was.

3

February 1, 2013.

I picked Gus up the next afternoon. One year earlier, to the day, I had put down the last of my three boxers. But now that door had closed, and another one had opened, with my new friend.

The feeling of elation swept me off my feet. I was a little worried about Gus, however. But, to my satisfaction, everything went smoothly.

It was a 20-mile ride back home, but it felt like I was spending glorious moments in timelessness with a long-lost friend. It was the first time Gus ever sat in my Trailblazer, and he made a noble effort at getting as comfortable as he possibly could.

We reached his new house, and he gladly let me help him out of the car. Gus was territorial, just like other dogs. He glanced around, found a spot toward the nearest bush, and marked his territory.

Although there were many dogs around in the neighborhood, Gus was exceptional, and he made it seem so, too. All the other dogs had finally known that a newcomer was here.

The first day together is always important. I believe it sets the tone for the relationship. Gus and I went inside the house. He took a good look around the house, and I could tell he was slightly hesitant and cautious.

Curious Gus weaved in and out of each room. His house speculation skills were so professional. He could teach anyone searching for a home a thing or two. I took him out to the backyard and walked him around the perimeter. I wanted to walk him through each section of the house. I wanted to honor him as a guest and a friend.

Once we were through the orientation, it was time for me to bathe Gus. Having picked up ticks from his time on the streets, Gus could use a good clean. I was slowly feeling like a pet owner, and Gus was making it all the more comfortable and indulgent. He knew what to do. He sat in the tub, lapped up water from the showerhead, and remained patient. I clipped his nails and cleaned his ears. And, in the midst of it all, I think I caught a glance of him smiling at me. We had entered a different time and space. The bath was empowering and meaningful—as if we washed away the bitter, bad memories of his past life. It felt like a clean slate, and I was going to do everything in my power to make Gus live like a king.

The bath did wonders. Gus's radiant fawn color had suddenly come to life. For a moment, as I stared into his big black eyes, it felt like a dream. Perhaps he felt the same too. He pranced around the bedroom, rolled on the carpet, all nice and clean. I chuckled at his antics and caressed his soft and shiny body. He then stood up and gazed directly into my eyes.

Those warm eyes that seemed so hollow and desperate just a few days earlier had now lit up—with love, gratitude, and happiness. My boy was feeling fine now. He took a good look at me, almost as if he didn't know how to thank me for saving him, giving him a home, and showing him a door to a new life. Perhaps at that point, I didn't know how to articulate how I felt for Gus, but he was already changing my life.

I also wanted Gus to see the pool. All my previous boxers had loved splashing in the water, and I assumed Gus would too. He came with me to check the pool out, just in case he ever wanted to swim—which, as it turns out, wasn't going to be anytime soon or ever actually.

Gus didn't look like he loved to swim. I accepted it. Well, initially. I will be honest—I did try once to get him to go in the pool. For some reason, I assumed he'd like it, as Lucy, the previous boxer I had.

My days with Lucy were incredibly memorable. She was one of the best boxers I had; she went to heaven much too soon. Lucy was quite eager to swim in the pool. She loved it so much, and her antics made me chuckle. Lucy would paddle in the water until she couldn't anymore. What was it about playing in the pool that appealed to her so much? I couldn't figure it out. But Lucy certainly had a special place in my heart.

With Gus, I thought hitting the pool would be just as satisfying. So, one day, I gently picked him up, cradled him in my arms while holding his back legs, and went in. His anxiety was visible, which is why we only went halfway. But it was an extraordinary experience for sure. I didn't know why Gus hated the pool. Was it something about the water? Did the depth scare him? Or was it something in his past that I was yet to find out? It was hard to answer all these questions, but I certainly knew one thing.

4

DOGS ARE LIKE humans. They came in all shapes and sizes and have starkly different and unique personalities. I realized that I could never force Gus into anything. He carried a separate identity, and I had to respect that. Living with him was going to be similar to the way I had lived with a partner. He brought many beautiful traits into my life. No matter what he did, he was always a gift.

Just gazing at him with warmth and tenderness, I realized how unique the idea of love is. Love can be a thousand things, but all of them mean nothing if you don't have anyone to share them with. Gus was the embodiment of the purest kind of love for me. I thought the windows to love in my life had been closed. In most cases, I had pushed love away because I was scared. But Gus gently tugged at my heart and slowly pulled me back to a new world-view. I don't mean to sound philosophical, but his arrival had stirred a "paradigm shift" in the way I had been looking and observing the world for so long.

As I had done with all my dogs, I took Gus for a check-up. I wanted to make sure that he was in good health before we started our new life together. I took him to my vet and got him thoroughly checked. Taking care of a pet and loving them means that you must do everything to keep them healthy and safe.

I was suspecting tick fever because of the significant number of ticks on his body. Even when I was positive at heart, I prayed hard that everything came out clear.

As we waited for the test results to come back, I decided to introduce Gus to my community over the next week or so. My neighborhood was always peaceful and quiet. Most of the people here were retirees, empty nesters, or other senior citizens. They were all wholesome people who, like me, were braving life in one way or the other.

I was a little hesitant, not knowing how the other dogs would react to Gus. But I had faith in him. Gus was different in the sense that he emitted incredible energy wherever he went. He was friendly and unique. Gus quickly struck a loving friendship with the dogs of the neighborhood—Chuck, Rocky, Will, and Grace—to name a few.

To this day, I don't know why this happened, really. But to see Gus blend in my community so quickly was nothing short of a delight. Everyone loved him. What more could I ask for?

Gus was my best pal. We went out for long walks that almost felt spiritual and life-giving for both of us. We spoke to each other in an unheard, unspoken language of love—there's so much purity and soulfulness to my feelings for Gus. Communicating with him was never hard. He understood me, and I knew what he wanted.

5

IN JUST A few days, Gus and I developed an unshakable bond. Having felt so lost, betrayed, and broken in life, it was undoubtedly a newfound trust. But the past didn't matter anymore. All that was important was right here in front of us. This bond between two souls was going to etch itself in the fabric of time.

His test results came back sooner than expected, and the news was what I had hoped. Thankfully, there was no tick fever.

While Gus and I were the same with emotions, I realized very soon our habits were quite the same as well. He was impressively disciplined—just the way I liked my pets. He never chewed at the furniture or relieved himself anywhere other than outside.

Our favorite time of the day was the night, when we could finally unwind. It was the calm hours of the night when I finally got a chance to lie by his side and stare into his beautiful, warm eyes. His beauty was overwhelming. As the night's silence grew, I always became more attentive to his undeniable innocence and beauty and often thought, "Who would have let you go?" "Why would anyone want to send you away?"

Was Gus a lost dog? Had he been owned by a little girl or boy who was desperately looking for their pet? I remember spending almost a month trying to find out if postings for Gus were on the internet. But I didn't find a single picture or plea. Soon enough, it was clear to me. Gus was mine. He was my pal. If he did have an owner, it didn't matter anymore. I was Gus's guardian now. I told Gus, "Nobody will separate us. I promise you that, and I love you."

I whispered those words in his ear—frequently, as a reassurance to myself. Gus always made sure to let me know he loved me back by giving me a big wet kiss with his tongue. He never disappointed me whenever I asked for his affection.

If I knew how to write poetry, I would have penned a thousand couplets for my boy. He was just that incredible. Somehow, he outshone the humans around me. Gus was prominent in my life, but I felt his presence especially when I was at work.

The company I worked for was small, and so was my office space. Bringing Gus with me to work was the most enjoyable part of the day. This guy made friends quickly in the office; I almost thought he was casting a magic spell. Gus was especially popular amongst my clients. One of them often brought in a dog named Ted. And, boy! Gus and Ted struck an undeniable friendship. As the dogs ran and chased each other, I saw the thirst for life, happiness, and vigor in Gus's eyes.

6

FROM A BROKEN, lonely dog to the happiest ball of sunshine, my pet's transformation was real. "You won't regret this," Gus had seemed to say when we shared an intimate gaze at the animal shelter. And, to this day, I haven't regretted a single moment. We spent each second, each minute, together. From doggy day camps to playing with other dogs and visiting family on a few occasions, Gus was like my right hand.

After about a year and a half, something stirred in me. I decided it was time for both of us to venture off, explore, and travel throughout the United States. The plan was to visit the West Coast, Canada, and finally Alaska, spending six months on the road. Then we would come back and settle in Illinois, where I had lived for 37 years.

My sole concern was to keep Gus safe, healthy, and happy. I knew well how to fend for myself, but I was worried about him. Nonetheless, I became super psyched for the adventure Gus and I were about to live.

I put my house on the market and sold it in three days. I put an ad on Craigslist and sold almost everything I had. The only items I kept were two bicycles, my clothes, and a toolbox. Gus and I would travel with very little to our name. The important thing was we were together. It was new for me to take such a bold step, but at this point in my life—especially with Gus around—I had somehow found the strength and impetus to go all in. Everything was slowly falling into place.

Soon after the sale of my house and figuring out the logistics of traveling, it became apparent that this might not be the best thing for Gus. Yes, he was young and healthy, but was this fair to him? It was my plan, my dream, but I needed to keep his best interests in mind, too. I decided to forego this bucket list item and stay put. The problem now, finding a place for us to live.

Gus and I found a small but super-cozy condo three miles away from where we had lived, fully furnished, beautiful, and indeed a blessing. Yes, it was compact, but that only made it even more comfortable for Gus and me. We moved in on August 1, 2013. I thought it would be tough, but I had moved several times in my life, so I had quite a bit of experience under my belt.

Gus and I were starting a new life, and I wanted nothing more than to see him happy. What made the new condo even better was the nearby park. Gus enjoyed his time in the park. The park was about 25 yards away and big enough for my boy to explore. The spy/agent he was, he left no stone unturned in exploring every nook and cranny of the park. He loved it. And I loved him.

The newness of the condo had slowly begun to seep in. We loved the small place because it only meant that Gus could always be under my eyes. I would often see him basking in the morning sun outside on the balcony. I don't want to sound cheesy, but my boy was no less than a ball of sunshine himself. He was pure happiness. I knew he loved the amber rays, so I would open the balcony door every day to let Gus out. He'd stretch and lie down on his blanket. He would close his eyes and feel the warmth of the sun on his body. The way Gus lived life was inspiring.

He compelled me to enjoy and bask in the beauty around me, too. I wanted to be in the present and feel the warmth of nature, just as Gus did. At that point, I may not have had a human companion, but I had a dog who taught me about life. He showed me all the beauty and joy that's hidden in the little things of life.

The simple act of gracefully walking out to enjoy the sunlight was a message from my dog. It was to untie the knots in my head, throw caution to the wind, and enjoy each day with warmth and gratitude.

Sometimes, the thoughts that came to me were so profound, I was compelled to grab my camera and snap a picture of Gus. Lying there, innocently engrossed in the sunshine, Gus was a beauty to admire. And, I wanted to capture his best moments because they were also my best moments.

Our days spent in the cozy condo were an absolute dream. I often caught Gus performing the wildest antics. Sometimes he tried to capture the slow-motion dust specks that swirled near the sunlit window. Other times, he would leap into my bed and wake me up to catch the sunrise. We enjoyed meals together and loved playing in the park as well. Each time he did something to make me chuckle, I would take a picture. My mind often wandered: "Who could have let this wonderful dog go?"

Who could, in their right mind, ever think that Gus was not worthy or drop him off in an open field to fend for himself? The thought shattered my heart, but I became even more adamant about giving Gus the best life every time it did. But I was going to face fears and challenges that I couldn't have foreseen.

As our time went by in the condo, I noticed Gus was behaving quite oddly. It was unlike him. Gus often stared down at the floor. He did it so often it began to worry me. The symptoms he showed were quite familiar to me. For some reason, the first thought that struck my mind was valley fever!

My baby boxer, Lucy, had had it. It was mild at first but then escalated to the level where it started to affect her muscles, causing severe limping at times. The toll it had taken on her health was heartbreaking. The illness crept in and mercilessly took her life. It started with a mild twitching in her head but soon ravaged her whole body. Lucy began experiencing seizures that were incredibly painful to watch. The seizures soon became a regular part of Lucy's life. No matter what we did, nothing would stop the disease from worsening every day.

The seizures also became more frequent and violent. They tested Lucy hard and challenged her will to live. Even thinking about it now sends a tingle down my spine. The fever was cruel. I still remember those painful moments when I had to leave Lucy for three days in the hospital. I'd stay by her side, caressing her belly, and whisper comforting words in her ear. But it broke me every time Lucy began shaking, battling the fever, and fighting for her life. I'd tell her, "My little girl, I will be back and will wait for you at the pool with your favorite ball."

Perhaps that was the only thought that gave Lucy and me the comfort we

yearned for—that we will return home and things will get back to normal. Lucy did come through, and she was able to go home. But things were never the same.

Eventually, the dark, gloomy day when Lucy began having seizures to a greater extent had approached. Her eyes told me that she had had enough. Her life had been complete. And even when it was tearing me apart, I knew it was time to let go. The pool at our house was going to miss her terribly, but it was time for her to enjoy splashing in heaven's beautiful waters. Lucy gently closed her eyes, and she finally breathed her last. Having suffered so much, I was at peace that she finally had the chance to rest.

My memories of Lucy were special, but they left a gaping hole in my heart. Once more, life had instilled a fear of losing someone I dearly loved. And, so, the same fear trickled into the present and terrified me. What if Gus was sick? But for now, it turns out he wasn't. And I was thankful for that.

For the rest of the year in the condo, Gus played around and grew fond of the area. By now, the trust between us was such that I could take him out without a leash. Like a dog who loved his freedom, he always seemed to wander a few feet from me, but Gus always knew he had to stay close. Gus was a good boy who behaved well.

He was a handsome dog and received compliments on the streets. One could tell that he knew he was good-looking because every time someone praised him, my boy would wag his tail and shake his butt until the passers-by smiled and laughed. Whenever other people approached him with awe and smiles, I would make sure to sit him by my side so that they could pet him. However, there were always a few people who felt a little uncomfortable when Gus walked without a leash. In that case, I would always put the leash on his collar.

I still remember this one day, a girl stopped in her tracks the moment she spotted Gus. She was so captivated with Gus that she didn't hesitate to ask me at once whether it was a coyote I was walking.

I laughed and shook my head. It was just my beautiful boxer named Gus; nothing more, just a friend, a companion, a soul mate who was going to make my days better and worth living. Gus almost instantly became friends with everyone he met. Not because he was playful, but for a big boxer, he was a gentle and calm dog. And it was perhaps this solace and maturity with a hint of playfulness on his face that pulled people toward Gus.

Our time at the condo was short-lived—only a year later, we set off to the Midwest.

7

ONCE AGAIN, WE left things behind us and headed out for our adventure. Considering that I had spent quite a lot of time in Illinois and Missouri, I decided to throw my resume to as many companies in these places as possible. The company that gave me the best offer would be the one I'd take off to, and to my surprise, it was Springfield, Missouri. The destination was 1,200 miles. So, I figured we could drive 300 miles a day. That would allow us to recover from the day's drive and arrive early enough to settle in our new place before I had to report to my new job. We could spend those moments bonding and loving life.

As our journey developed and matured, I realized that we were about to create our new life in Missouri. There was something about Missouri that pulled me toward this place. The last time I had visited Missouri was for a wedding in the summer of 2014.

Driving from one state to the other with Gus by my side was nothing short of a delight. Gus was a natural at traveling in the car. I had expected him to loosen up a bit and relax, but to my surprise, he called shotgun. He sat straight in the front seat of the car and didn't move at all. The sight even astonished a few passers-by. Each time I was unsure, I'd just stick my hand for that very special paw shake. That was my way of knowing Gus was okay.

I loved that Gus sat up in front with me. I would caress his belly, keep shaking his paws, and frequently rest my arm around him. It was my way of letting Gus know how much I cherished and enjoyed his company. This journey was going to be incredibly momentous for both of us. It would be a time to develop loving memories and an unshakable bond with each other.

Now that I think about it, I can safely say that our journey to the Midwest was honestly a blast and one of the best memories I had with him. During the drive, our first stop was Texas, and shortly afterward, Springfield, Missouri. It was here when we moved into our third house together. The place was

peaceful, beautiful, and nostalgic. A cedar tree stood on one side while a big oak tree covered the front yard.

The house was big but needed a good cleaning and a bit of DIY yard renovation. So, I trimmed the trees, mowed the grass, and tried to spruce up the outdoors as much as possible. The cutting of the grass brought back fond memories of living on a farm back in Morris Illinois, during my teenage and college years. Who knew I'd be at it again, years later, with Gus?

I always enjoyed cutting the grass. It gave me a sense of calm and pleasure. Gus enjoyed his new backyard as well. He would lie on his back and bask in the sun. I kept a close eye on him, but I wasn't the only one. Our new neighbors had quickly grown fond of him. As was the case everywhere else we had been, more than me, Gus took the initiative and made the most friends.

Gus and I were now in a lovely place together. The beautiful country life was slowly growing on us, and we loved and cherished each moment of it. Although August was a particularly hot month, it only reminded me of how much I had admired the country lifestyle. The fresh air, the sneaky squirrels chirping and sprinting up the trees, and the warm sun was just the perfect life. And what made it special was that I wasn't alone. These were perhaps the best days of my life, and they were all being shared with my compassionate and loving dog, Gus.

He loved the yard the same way I did. I quickly realized that perhaps the main reason we clicked so instantly was that we had the same habits and preferences. As humans, we don't think about this much, but we meet people who end up sparking joy for life in our hearts. In my case, it wasn't a human that endowed the gift and blessings of life to me. It was Gus.

My neighbors loved Gus. In the backyard, he ran without a leash. The smile on his face as he leaped and ran from one corner to the other was always of pure delight. One of my neighbors to the south of our house came over and introduced herself. Edith was quick on her toes and always had a beat on what was happening in the neighborhood. I had struck a good friendship with her. We went to Sunday church together, and she'd always make it a point to inform me about every shenanigan that happened in our little neighborhood. Sometimes it was a bit unsettling. But on most days, she made me chuckle. Edith often delivered roadside sermons to me, which I didn't mind; however, her husband, I felt, was more in need of some traditional teaching than I was. But he was quite friendly. He stopped often and jokingly nagged me to stop doing so much work in the yard.

It only gave his wife the chance to lecture him about his yard duties. But that's how we became friends. We started a friendly barter system, where I trimmed his trees and mowed his yard, and he'd return the favor by hauling off the branches and grass clippings from my yard.

The neighbor adjacent to me was an elderly widow. She was very well-spoken and was always working outside in her yard. We would say hello to each other and spend a few minutes chatting while working in our yards. Her husband had been the pastor of the local church. Other people in the neighborhood also had close ties with the church. Safe to say, I was living in a decent, homespun community.

8

WITH ALL ITS perks, the neighborhood wasn't always a friendly place, however. While tidying up the lawn one day, I decided to visit my neighbor down the street. As someone particular about their yard, I was bothered by this overgrown, disheveled lawn. I wanted to tidy up their yard so that it could look beautiful, crisp, and clean. But this neighbor was someone I had never met. I had only seen her getting in and out of the car.

I thought to myself that if I mowed her lawn, she'd like it. I mean, I didn't see anyone else helping her, and so I cleaned up her yard. I mowed the grass, trimmed the shrubs, and pulled the weeds.

However, when I finished the work, cleaned up, and began to settle down at home, I heard the doorbell ring. To my surprise, it was a man. He briefly interrogated me on whether I was the one who cleaned up the lady's lawn. As I nodded, his eyebrows furrowed. He looked upset.

The man warned me never to go to her house again. She was a very private person and didn't like being bothered. I was taken aback for a moment and glanced over at Gus. Despite the lengthy explanation, I realized quickly that my kindness wasn't received very well. So, I shut the door and called Gus over. My boy came running into my arms and looked at me intensely. It was almost as if he was telling me "I told you so."

Fall had arrived and the raking of the leaves began. Gus and I loved admiring the auburn leaves and the freshly cut grass. Gus would lie on the concrete and snuggle into his soft blanket. The best friend that he was, Gus also made sure to supervise and check if I did all my chores correctly.

During this time of the season, the snakes and the rodents often came out. The latter were easy to live with, but I feared the snakes the most.

When I would cut the grass, Gus, on occasion, would witness me jumping and screaming, trying to dodge a snake, and he would immediately come to my rescue. He'd bark and dance around and make sure to give the snake a good scare. I was so proud of him. He'd do his work and confidently walk out of the scene—like an actor who knew he did an excellent job.

He even tried chasing this one particular rabbit. Gus was so competitive. The chase had consumed him completely. It didn't matter that he was almost out of breath, that he ended up banging his head on the fence, or that his eyes bulged out every time he chased the rabbit. He just wanted to be victorious. Over the next few months, he had many encounters with possums, rabbits, and snakes. At first, I was a little fearful and wanted to protect him. But he was ever-so-valiant and handled every critter that seemed to bother him.

Even when he seemed like he was in visible danger, he stood tall and strong, with his chest out. He was a boxer after all, and boxers never falter. Perhaps, in his little ways, Gus was trying to teach me how to be courageous myself.

9

WEEKS HAD GONE by, and the fall season was coming to a close. Winter was setting in. I wondered if this was Gus's first winter. I assumed it would be, so I wanted to make it memorable and welcoming as possible. Winter wasn't my favorite season, but the fireplace we had would provide many cozy and memorable nights.

Gus and I ventured out for firewood for our place. Living in Arizona, my eyes had been accustomed to a desert setting. Yet, Missouri had a charm of its own. And by now, Gus and I had embraced most of it. Our long trips to collect firewood were delightful, if not sense-tingling experiences. We watched birds of every kind and color, adorable chipmunks playing, and squirrels making their way up the trees. The life around us was feeding our souls. It was so much more than what I had imagined.

The first frost had arrived, and I was happy to witness Gus's expression. He marveled at the white, glistening snow and tiptoed over it as if he was walking on ice crystals that would crack if he put too much weight on the ground. I could tell it was his first snow, and I tried my best to reassure him. I wanted him to know that the snow would welcome him and that he could always sink his paws into the snowy blanket that would fall over the yard. That all the life around him—the birds, the snow, the grass—loved him the way I did. I wanted to show him that he made this world a beautiful place.

Gus started liking winter, and we continued enjoying our time together outdoors. He was playful in the snow and rolled around it like it was his bed. At times, he'd roll around so furiously that he'd have a snow beard on his face when he got up. It was so much fun to watch. He was my own little Santa.

Despite this being Gus's first winter, he did an impressive job. I was most grateful to him for not falling sick. During our winter walks, as our feet sunk into the snow, I would pick Gus up anytime I sensed that he felt excessively cold. I'd open up my winter jacket and cradle my boy inside it. It was his time to get warmed up and be as close to me as possible. And we both loved every bit of that closeness.

Every day, after dinner, I would build a fire. We'd get comfortable, throwing a few oversized pillows and blankets on the floor. I'd read a book as the fire crackled beside us. We'd fall asleep as the gentle flames warmed up our bodies. I didn't realize how Gus's presence and companionship had planted a seed of gratitude in me. Every day that I'd wake up and see Gus by my side, my heart would give thanks. I didn't have riches or blessings in the "conventional" sense, but God had given me an incredible dog who reminded me why I'm alive.

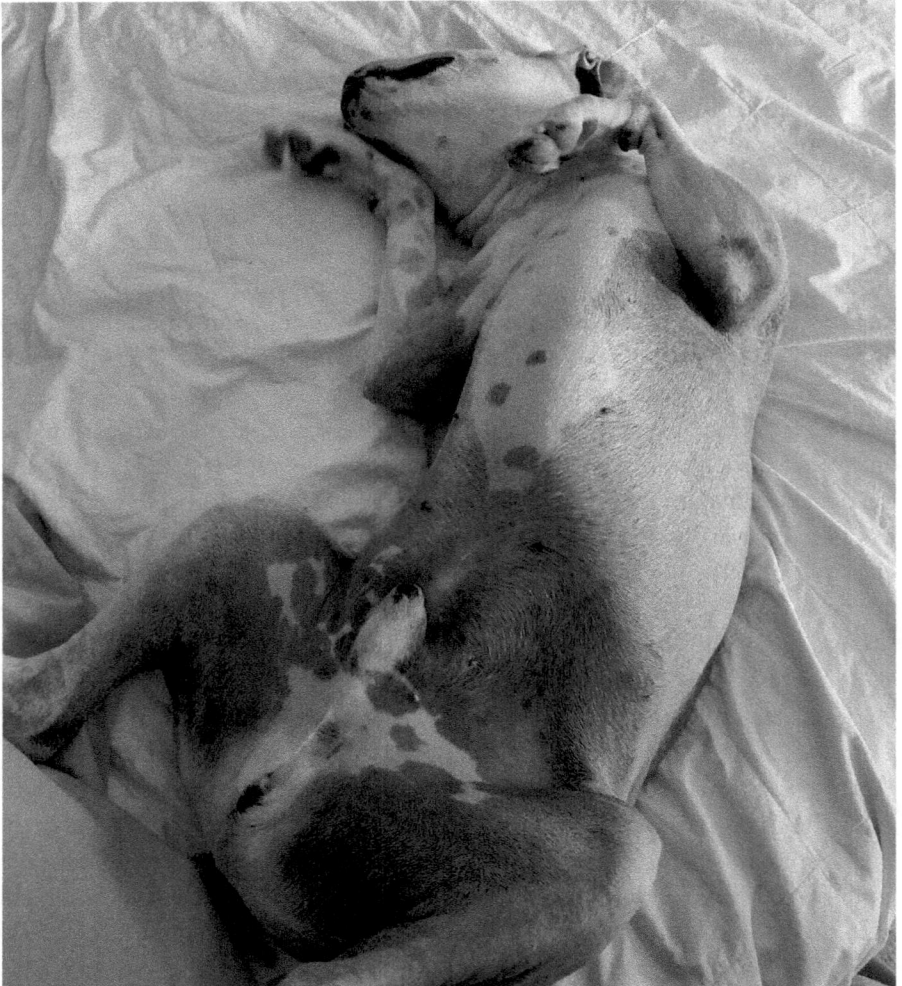

10

ONCE THE HOLIDAYS were over, I decided to move back to Arizona. Little did I know that this was going to be one of the most meaningful and consequential decisions of my life. Arizona has a place in my heart for countless reasons. I had been contemplating this decision for a while, and I couldn't wait to get back.

Now that we had savored Missouri's beauty, I put in my two-week notice in early March. The only thing I knew I was going to miss about Missouri was the backyard. It kept me busy for most of the day, and somehow, Gus and I had developed a routine too. The yard gave both of us so much to look forward to; we both would miss it. Its radiant beauty during the fall season was a sight to behold. I was also going to miss the beautiful friendships I had made, especially with Patti—a woman I had met at work. She was one person who'd always be a part of my life.

And, as I did before moving to Missouri, I sold everything. Thankfully, my neighbors ended up buying all my yard equipment and furniture. There was some firewood left from the time Gus and I had collected it, and I gave that to a family in the neighborhood. My journey out of Missouri was going to be just as smooth and hassle-free as when I first came. And, with Gus by my side, it was going to be time well-spent. During all this time, as luck had it, I managed to get my old job back and moved back to the furnished condo I was in before I left for Missouri.

For the momentous journey to Arizona, we were going to be hauling back a 1966 Chevy Impala convertible. I had purchased this beauty from a dealer in Kansas shortly before the winter began. I had had a love and passion for vintage cars ever since I had seen my childhood friend, Terry, own one. He owned a '66 Super Sport with a sky-blue exterior and a slightly darker blue interior. It was a sweet ride and inspired my taste in cars.

At this point, I didn't know how to get two vehicles and a moving truck to Arizona. I figured the truck was not needed, so I decided to donate it. We drove the Impala to the truck rental place and loaded the car onto the trailer. My boy jumped into the passenger seat as we headed back for our last night in the house.

I will never forget that night. It was long, quiet, and sweet. Gus and I bid farewell to our memorable moments, which would stay in our hearts forever. In hindsight, our time in Missouri was also crucial because I had bonded with Gus in a way I never had a chance to.

We had moved from a condo to a big house. We had learned how to blend into the new neighborhood, how to make new friends, how to have fun by ourselves. Together we had learned and adapted. I was there for him when he was in danger, and he was there for me when I needed someone to kick some sense into me. And I wouldn't have had it any other way.

That night, we took our last walk around the block. I knocked on our neighbors' doors and we paid our hearty goodbyes. We wanted to make sure not to leave anyone out, even those who had been distant.

We then went back to our house. I still remember as I ushered Gus in and closed the door, the muffled silence caught my heart like a hook. I stood in one place for a long time and had a good look at the house. I wanted to savor and memorize each corner of that place. Every single thing about that house was memorable and meaningful to me. The little spot by the fireplace where the soft flames embraced us in their warmth, that bright red rug near the back door that Gus would be sitting on when I would return home for lunch during my work week. That lovely, achingly beautiful backyard that we built and nurtured together—the memories were all too vivid.

That night, we slept on the floor, our bodies huddled against each other, our heads sunk into the soft pillows and blankets to keep us warm. It was a bittersweet night, but as long as I had my boy with me, everything was okay.

11

MONDAY MORNING CAME, and the chirping of the birds pleasantly awakened me. I lifted the blanket next to me, but Gus wasn't there. He was up before me. He jumped up and down as I got up, ushering me to get on with the day's work. And I certainly had some essential things to do. I met with the landlord to return the keys and the garage door opener and to walk through the house for final approval. To my surprise, he gave me all of my security deposit back. He appreciated my efforts in keeping the yard extra clean and tidy. He loved how well I had maintained the house despite living with a pet. I thanked him for his generosity, and off we went.

I was excited for our journey to Arizona. For me, it was going to be quite a nostalgic event. I was returning to the small family-owned company and the old neighborhood. Luckily, I had managed to transmit some of this excitement into Gus as well. His demeanor was resolute and decisive—after all, we were heading off on a significant venture.

However, I wasn't sure how well I'd be able to drive, considering I had to pull the car. Luckily, hauling the '66 Chevy on a trailer wasn't a hefty task at all. The plan was to drive for six hours and stop to rest for the night. This way, I'd have enough energy to complete the journey and look after Gus.

I wanted to give Gus a comfy seat in the car, so I piled many blankets and pillows in the passenger seat—this journey was just as important to him as it was to me.

The truck was much more comfortable and easy to handle than previous moving trucks I had used. Somehow, it felt as if everything was falling into place.

Gus and I were now gearing up for a new road and a new life. I don't quite remember where we made our first pit stop. However, it was quite farther than the six-hour limit I had initially planned. Gus was yet again a rock star at traveling. During those six hours, he'd sit in the passenger seat, the window open, and his ears flapping in the wind.

Since I couldn't move into my condo until the next few days, Gus and I had plenty of time to make the drive. So, we decided to stop and rest for a while. The anticipation of returning to Arizona and going back to my job, the same condo and neighborhood, psyched me up. All the pieces were finally falling into place. My life hadn't made sense in a long time. And, this time, I felt something was right. My choices were correct. This time, I had an angel by my side to guide me and bless my decisions. And, that angel was Gus.

I felt invigorated. After all, there's no place like home, and Arizona was mine. Somehow, I felt powerful energy and vigor to keep driving. Occasionally, I'd look to my side and admire, as Gus would raise his paw for a shake, as if telling me that I was doing a fantastic job driving the truck.

When we stopped for a rest, Gus left his markings, letting the other dogs know that he had been there. The sky was clear, and there was an unusual sense of calm and quiet. Soon after, we hopped in the truck, and the second leg of our journey began. This time, I drove for 13 hours straight. I couldn't believe the energy and zest that was firing up inside of me. Somehow, I wanted to cover the miles as soon as I could. We had been on the road for such a long time. We did make a few stops on the route to grab some food and stretch our legs, but that was it.

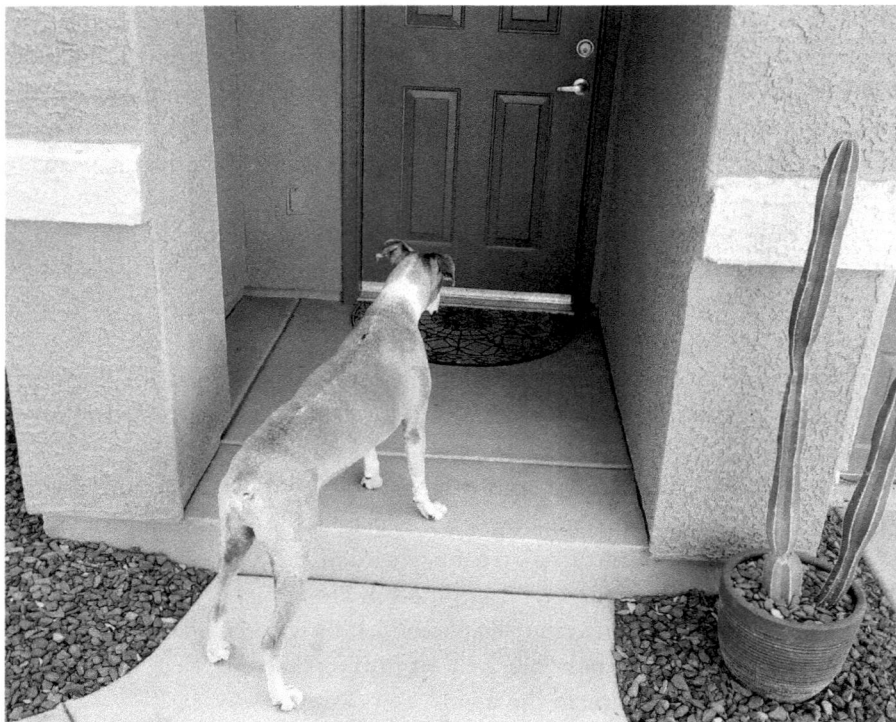

It's different when you're traveling with a human. With a dog who doesn't know how to express their needs, I knew the responsibility was far more pressing. Before we knew it, we had arrived in Flagstaff, about two hours from our destination. Suddenly, I decided that perhaps spending another two hours on the road wouldn't be that difficult.

It was around midnight when we arrived. I was excited, so I drove right to the condo, found a parking spot, and parked my car across the street. We eagerly jumped out of the truck. It seemed that Gus was in more of a hurry than I was. He almost leaped out of the truck. I could feel the crispness of the air. The place was so familiar to my senses. Suddenly, everything became overwhelming to me.

Gus and I slowly paced around the park across from the condo. But I had to keep reminding myself that all this was new for Gus. There was nothing familiar about this place to him. His excitement and eagerness to explore the new area were delightful. My feelings of nostalgia and his emotions of discovering a new place had intertwined beautifully.

My boy began sniffing the new scents. The earthy smell of the grass and the dirt had quickly caught him. He began marking his territory to let everyone know he was back in town. That night I was the happiest soul. We were going to nap for a few hours before daylight..

12

THIS WAS THE perfect time to make use of my Chevy. I moved the bench seat as forward as I could, grabbed all the blankets and pillows, and prepared the coziest open-roof bed for the both of us. It was certainly long enough and big enough for both of us to snuggle together. I called for Gus, and he jumped in, and I shut the car's door.

The night was quiet, serene, and breathtaking. My boy and I cuddled against one another—the same way we did near the fireplace in Missouri. At that point, I wondered why I didn't get a hotel room. However, the answer was clear. A night spent in a hotel can never beat the beauty of the sky that Gus and I were experiencing. We were nature lovers. Our souls were of the same elements.

The blankets kept us warm. I rubbed Gus's belly and told him that I loved him and that we were home. He raised his paw in approval, letting me know that he was fine. Something about that night was magical because when I uttered the words, "Gus, I love you," I felt a tingle down my spine. I felt a promise birthing in my heart. If I had nine lives, Gus was going to be a companion in all of them. He was my savior, and I was his. We were made for each other. Gus was always and forever going to be my boy.

Lying in the back seat, with my boy cuddled up next to me, his paw in my hand, feeling his heartbeat with mine, I knew I was where I was supposed to be. Now that I think of it, this was perhaps, the most memorable moment I had with Gus. Lying in my car with my dog made me realize that real joy and happiness were not in the big, grandiose things in life. They were in the simple things. Gus was a simple dog. But he was my world.

The morning was chilly and came quickly. My vision was hazy, as I tried to recognize my surroundings. It was almost as if I was waking up from a sweet dream. Gus, lying on the pillows, moved a little and nudged at me. I looked over to his side as he crawled out of the blankets. I regained my senses slowly, and we both stretched our legs. Despite the chilly morning, I could see Gus smiling at me, and that was all the warmth I needed.

The sun was shining bright. I knew it was going to be a beautiful start to the day. My boy and I took a quick walk through the neighborhood. We wanted to get familiar with the people, the parks, and the stores. As we strolled inside the community complex, I felt a tingle of nostalgia run down my spine. Not much had changed since the eight months we were away. And I was glad. Everything from the parks and baseball fields to the beautiful houses was the same as when we had left. We were hungry, so I grabbed some food for Gus and myself.

I got some delicious kibble for Gus and bought a sandwich for myself. Of all the meals I've shared with someone, my time spent eating with my boy was one that I cherished. As he hastily munched on his food, I couldn't help but admire the pure happiness, joy, and sincerity this dog had brought into my life. I knew he was a godsend.

My thoughts wandered off to all the things we had gone through in the last two years. The feelings overwhelmed me, and I couldn't help but envelop Gus in my embrace. The kibble in his mouth almost fell out because the hug was so tight. I gave him a kiss for being such a great companion, getting a small taste of his kibble.

We had a couple more hours before the landlady would show up and let us into our new place. I decided to take Gus for another ride to see some parts of the town. We drove around town and went past our old house. That house was so important to me. It had given me some of the most meaningful experiences of my life. Traveling in the old neighborhood was undoubtedly a beautiful reminiscence.

As we drove, I met an old neighbor on our way. He seemed surprised to see me back in town. Thankfully, he received us with kind words. I needed those words. I had entered my old town as a new person and, this time with Gus by my side. The kindness and the warm welcome were appreciated. He even gave Gus a big hug.

After that delightful encounter, I picked up some coffee and headed back to the condo to meet the landlady. She was warm, kind, and had so much compassion in her eyes. We were back in the condo and our move was officially over. It was easier and simpler this time because I didn't have as many belongings or possessions. Just a few things, and Gus. He was, after all, my most important possession.

Once we were in the condo, he went straight to the couch and lay there, just like old times. It was time to sort out all of our stuff. Although this wasn't

going to be much of a hassle, I still wanted to make sure I was tending to both Gus and myself. My boy didn't like riding in the car the way he loved the truck. But for now, I needed both time and money to buy a new vehicle for us.

The daily drive was going to be slightly tough. It was 18 miles one way and getting nine miles to the gallon in the Chevy, gas would become very expensive. If I were to come home for lunch and let Gus out, that would add another 200 miles a week.

I had to buy a new vehicle. There was no way Gus and I could take on the sweltering summer heat since the '66 didn't have any air conditioning. The moment you would hop in, the car would feel like a boiler. I decided to purchase a trendy Honda Fit. It was nice, compact, and perfect for the two of us. It also had great gas mileage and was an easy purchase. I had to sell the Impala to buy the new car. And it slowly hit me that I had always planned to buy an eight-track tape player and install it in the Impala. Gus and I would cruise the streets playing rock and roll with the top down. Gus and I had already seen and felt so much together. We had moved nearly three times, traveled long miles together—as much as 2,400 miles by now—that nothing seemed difficult when he was by my side. If anything, his presence made decisions easier for me.

By now, we were welcoming springtime. It was neither too cold nor too hot and it also meant that Gus and I could enjoy playing in the park. We took every chance we could to venture out for long walks, explore new areas, and play on the fresh grass.

It had only been a few days when I ran into my old friend, Debbie. Since my time away, Debbie had lost her beloved dog. Whenever I met someone who had lost their pet or something that reminded me of how I lost Lucy, I was jolted by a bitter realization that my relationship with Gus wasn't going to be forever.

It killed me to ever imagine a life without him.

Debbie was delighted to see us. She was a bit surprised as well. She mentioned that she saw someone outside walking their dog without a leash, thinking how wonderful that must feel, not knowing that Gus and I were returning from our sabbatical to the Midwest. It was a short and sweet encounter. Debbie had always been a dear friend. Over the next few days, Gus and I drove around in the convertible trying to explore and spot as many parks to play in and community corners to relax in as we could. It was going to be our home for a while so I wanted Gus to settle in properly. We had moved around so often in such a short while, I just wanted Gus to have a place to stay and to have the best life possible. But every time I felt like the constant moving was getting too much for my boy, Gus always reassured me. It seemed as if he didn't care much about where we lived, as long as we were together.

13

MY WORK WOULD commence the following Monday. I was excited to go back to my job but that meant I wouldn't be able to see Gus for at least six hours. I planned on coming home daily for lunch and letting him out, but we were still going to be apart for a long time. Oh, how I wished I could bring him to work with me.

I started leaving for work at 6:00 a.m. and would get back home around 11:30 to take him out for his break and to feed him lunch. Even in Missouri, I would make the drive home for lunch every day to take care of him. I am sure he could have lasted the ten hours until I came home from work, but I am not sure I could have. I think it was more for me, going home to see him, than anything else.

When you start living with someone, their presence becomes so natural to you. It's a beautiful and quiet acceptance that someone has carved a place in your heart. Gus had done that. But he was always a step ahead in loving me. Despite being so used to each other's presence, he would always welcome me with excitement and eagerness. Whenever he heard the click of the door, whether at lunch or the end of my day at work, he would always greet me at the landing of the stairs, wagging his tail and meeting me halfway down the stairs.

I would chase him up and he would jump on the couch and I would follow him. We almost always embraced each other in a playful hug and I always caught myself whispering "I love you" to my boy.

He gave me a kind of love I had never had before. Sometimes, I couldn't tell who was happier to see the other when I would walk in the door for lunch or return after work. In this relationship of pet and owner, sometimes the lines blurred and all that remained were two souls who loved each other very much.

We had a ritual every morning before I left for work. As I got ready, Gus would lie on the bed, snuggling with the sheets. When it was time for me to leave, I would roll him over on his back and give him a belly rub.

By this, he'd know that it was time for me to leave. Gus would prop up on his hind legs, alert and a little sad. He'd put his paws on my shoulders and I'd give him a big hug. We did this every day. After all, he was the best part of my day—whether I was bidding farewell in the morning or returning home by evening. My day practically revolved around Gus.

We had spent a few months in our condo. By now, Gus knew the way to each store and park in the neighborhood. He was smart and attentive. If human, Gus would've been the complete package—loving, compassionate, handsome, and intelligent. But he was a dog. There were days when I felt so lucky to have him. The feelings were so overwhelming.

His unbeatable loyalty, compassion, and love were unlike any other. No matter what happened, I knew I had Gus there to comfort me after a tiring day. My dog was indeed my best friend in every sense of the word.

Soon, it was summertime, and the heat was moving in. I never liked the humidity, but I could always welcome the warmth. We did experience an occasional swarm of mosquitos around the house, usually after a rain, but that was manageable with some repellent and a quick hand to swat them away. I think Gus liked it, too. He wasn't a picky or fussy dog. He adjusted quickly to the changing seasons, a quality about him that I grew to admire immensely.

We had the same routine, but sometimes, when it was sweltering hot, our walks would be shorter so that we could return to the condo without getting overheated. Our early strolls, well before the sun rose, seemed to be the best time for walking. Summertime, the temperature by 6:00 a.m. could reach into the triple digits.

The feel of the heat and sun on my body made my skin feel like it was burning. I could only imagine what Gus was feeling. This weather would only last about three months and eventually would subside. We were slowly learning to appreciate each season of our lives.

14

My job and my daily and weekly routines had become a set pattern. I would run into Debbie quite often, mostly on our walks or while hanging out in the park. We were chatting more often, and I don't exactly remember when, but in one of our conversations, she offered to walk Gus on Thursdays and Fridays. Although this meant that I wouldn't see my boy at lunchtime, I still took the offer because Gus would have some company. I trusted Debbie and had full faith in her that she would look after Gus as her own. She was an excellent dog owner. And, so, I gave her the key to my condo. I don't trust people easily, but her warm and trust-worthy disposition compelled me to trust her with the most valuable thing in my life.

Debbie was now taking Gus to the parks. She soon realized how great a walker Gus was. He never had to be put on a leash, and she realized that he was one of the very few dogs who was able to walk without a leash. Gus was always so well-behaved. It sometimes amazed me and made me feel incredibly lucky. I had grown used to walking him without a leash.

However, one afternoon, Gus and I were walking by a ravine in our complex. Gus was ambling by my side. He always knew his boundaries and was well aware that he had to stay close. However, this time something happened that caught me by surprise. Gus had spotted a coyote some 40 yards away or so from where we were walking. The once-vacant land was now being taken over by a new residential development of condominiums. Coyotes, along with other animals, were forced out in search of a new place to shelter.

Gus felt a strong instinct to chase the coyote, the same way he chased rabbits. The moment I caught him picking up his speed, I called his name. But he had already taken off in a hurry. I knew this could spell danger for Gus. So, I screamed and ran after him, waving my arms at him as he led me into the street. The road we lived on was quite busy and boisterous. I had to make sure that no cars were coming at Gus. I ran and ran. At some point, I couldn't even feel my legs. Thankfully, Gus realized that he wasn't going to catch the coyote. Gus immediately turned back as if realizing what he had just put me through. I was so exhausted that all I could say was, "You can still run for an old man, but let's not see how fast I can run anymore." I'll be honest; Gus challenged every inch of muscle in my body that day.

I embraced him and we continued on our walk. Whenever I strolled in the parks or along the streets with Gus, it almost felt like I was walking a human being, one with a mind and heart of their own. I never felt like a pet owner. Sometimes, it felt as if it was Gus who was leading us. I'd be walking on my own often to find Gus farther down the street. At first, it didn't make sense to me. I would wonder why Gus would not walk with me and why he would stop in his tracks and enjoy standing still while I kept on walking.

I'd look at him for a few seconds, expecting and waiting for him to follow me. He would look at me, too. Our eyes would communicate, and I would sense him telling me, "I think we should go this way." And I would readily agree with him because, somehow, I believed he knew the way better than I did. So, I'd often give in, turn around, and follow his route.

Most of the people who witnessed this often laughed and smiled at us. I'd smile back at them. I was more than happy to follow my boy. All of our walks back to the house were like a profound journey for Gus. He would explore, look around, gaze at anything that caught his attention, and sniff all the scents that came his way. The familiarity of the place, the streets, the air, and the thick grass was slowly making him feel at home. And yet, there were days when we would find something new to behold. I, on the other hand, loved to admire his journey from the periphery. So, it was an unspoken rule that Gus took the lead when we walked because to see him experience and feel the world around him was my favorite part of the day.

It was crazy how time flew. We had been back in Arizona for almost a year now. A new year awaited us: 2016. I felt an urge to start dating again. It had been three years since my divorce. My past relationship had so consumed me emotionally and mentally that, for a long while, I didn't have any zest and enthusiasm for life. With Gus in my life, I was slowly coming back to who I was. And, so I decided that I was ready to date and to explore this aspect of companionship one more time.

One of my friends encouraged me to sign up for a dating website. I signed up on one of those many dating websites that promise everlasting love and happiness. Even though nothing seemed promising, I wanted to give it at least three months and see how things turned out. You never know when luck might strike. I was looking for someone who didn't want to commit to a serious relationship—casual dating, as they called it. At that point in my life, I felt a sense of contentment. But I knew a partner could make it better. I had decided early on that I wouldn't put too much effort into it. I was just going to put myself out there so the right person would know enough about me to approach me. That was my only goal.

Those three months were indeed something. I had a chance to chat with many women with different lifestyles, backgrounds, and opinions. I loved exploring my preferences, and eventually, I ended up meeting someone who lived a few miles from where I lived. We hit it off and dated for a month or two, but in the end, it was clear I wasn't able to connect with her. My feelings weren't as profound. It wasn't that I decided to pull away quickly. One month, I feel, is a good time to gauge whether someone is right for you. And she wasn't.

15

However, throughout the time I dated, I never once left Gus alone. I had set my mind never to do that to my pal. When I did date, I made sure never to be away from Gus overnight. It made me happy that we could be together more often. My ultimate devotion had always been to Gus. He was the center of my world, and I never wanted any of my dates to disrupt our precious relationship.

My approach might have sounded rigid and unreasonable to some people, but I had my reasons. It wasn't that I feared a romantic commitment or was obsessed with Gus. My dog had introduced me to an extraordinary kind of love—a love I knew well that no human could have given me. And the peace, joy, and pure happiness I felt with him by my side was precious to me. I didn't want to give this up. I knew in my heart that dating would never fill the void that Gus's love and companionship had filled. So, I put my foot down whenever Gus needed me because, in many ways, I needed him more.

Gus had opened up my heart and had shown me that no feeling is final. My hopelessness and utter defeat had been a fleeting phase that I had had the strength to overcome. Gus was that special angel who had helped me get back on my feet again. My relationship with him was more substantial, unlike any I had experienced with a human in the past. So, I wanted to cherish and protect our bond.

I wasn't ready for a full-time commitment with a woman because my life was busy already. I didn't want to jump into that life anytime soon. So, when dating didn't quite work out for me, I decided to create a bucket list and use my leisure time to check off each item on it. I shifted my attention from dating to finally getting myself to do things I always wanted to do.

The first item was to train for and finish an Ironman Race. Ironman is considered the single most challenging one-day sporting event there is. It consists of 2.4 miles of swimming, 112 miles of biking, and 26.2 miles of running. Now, even recalling those days gives me goosebumps.

The race had a time limit of 17 hours for completion. There was a set time to complete each discipline. If you failed to complete each one by the cut-off time, you couldn't continue the race.

At the time, I honestly didn't know if I could do it. But the excitement of finding out what I was capable of was an intriguing thought, one that eventually consumed me. It's one of those times when I found the intrinsic satisfaction of enjoying my self-growth. Instead of searching for answers or love from other human beings, I was looking inward. And, I think in many ways, it was Gus who inspired me to become that way.

I knew I had to endure injuries, cramps, and hours of suffering to finish the race. But I was up for the challenge. Something was changing inside of me, and I was ready to embrace the person I was becoming. Plus, it wasn't that I was entirely new to triathlon. I had completed a few sprint triathlons back in 2010 and 2011. They were, however, not as big, but in a way, I had an idea of what to expect.

The decision to take up the race was significant. It would take hours and weeks of training before I could be physically capable of completing the race. So, one of my top priorities was not to neglect Gus in the process. I knew I couldn't do all of this alone, so I wanted a professional to hold me accountable for my progress until next year. So I decided to hire a coach to give me weekly schedules that I could follow. The race would be difficult and a big challenge, as I also had to juggle between working full time and training 10 to 20 hours a week. Things seemed a little bleak, and the challenge was daunting. But I was ready to push my limits and discover the unknown. Initially, I decided to aim for the half Ironman race in Cabo San Lucas. It was a short seven months away and would be a tune-up for the real competition that was going to take place in Florida the following April.

Throughout this time, I also had to think about Gus. There would be days when I would have to leave him for hours to get my training in. I wish he could have been with me on all my training runs and bike rides. On days I would ride my trainer indoors, his presence motivated me and pushed me to become the best version of myself. Any goal that I had aspired to achieve would be incomplete without Gus's presence and approval.

Based on my previous experiences of physical training, cycling had always been one of my strengths. For most of my life, I had been a bicycler more than a runner. So, I knew the wheels were my power. Swimming, however, was something I had never practiced enough to become anything more than an average swimmer. It would never become my strength, so I was hesitant about it from the start.

My training began slowly. It wasn't as aggressive as I had expected, but it was admittedly quite painful. I didn't realize how much my muscles ached until I began training continuously for hours. I had neglected my body for so long. I weighed 230 pounds. At the time, it was hard to regain all that strength, but I nonetheless pushed myself. Whenever I felt like giving up or slacking, I would look at Gus, who would immediately jump and leap around me as if to tell me I must never stop.

My training schedule was six to seven days a week, while every third week was my recovery period. It was a good routine. It was back-breaking and challenging. By my first recovery week, I was feeling pretty good. I set up my bike trainer inside the house so that I could ride it indoors. This way, I had more time to spend with Gus.

16

THANKFULLY, MY COMPLEX had a gym, so a treadmill was always accessible. Joining a gym that had a pool was essential because I needed to hone my skills at swimming, my weakest discipline. In a few weeks, I could see that my training schedule was finally coming together. I had an impeccable and effortless routine that I would leap into right after waking up. Now that I was finally doing something I wanted, I couldn't have felt more elated.

Within a month, I had reached a few milestones. I lost a significant amount of weight and was finally starting to see the results. This race taught me many things, and one of them was to focus on consistency more than anything. I knew then that the results would follow. The fact that I had lost so many pounds helped further in cycling, running, and swimming with greater flexibility. I could move my body how I wished without fearing an ache in my back or legs.

My schedule became predictable. My week would start with swimming, followed by a bike day and then a run day. Some weeks, I would have a day off, some weeks it was training all seven days. Saturdays would be my long bike day, with Sunday being my long run day. My coach's goals became easier but also more difficult as the weeks of training went by.

The training was intense and challenged every inch of my body. My body was always feeling super-charged. Time was flying by and I didn't even realize that my high school reunion was looming soon. I wished to take a break from the workouts and meet a few of my good old friends from back in the day. The last reunion I had attended was in 1991, my tenth—what a glorious time it was.

I was genuinely excited at first, but something urged me to stay back as the date got closer. Yes, I wanted to reunite and catch up with old friends, but times were different now. I decided that my training was more important to me than meeting people I hadn't seen in 25 years. I knew that I had to show commitment to what was in front of me. I couldn't let my heart or mind relent for even a second.

After Gus, training for this race was monumental. I had to push myself in every way, to hopefully beat the time I set for myself to complete this race. I didn't want to attend the reunion because I didn't want to be away from Gus for the week I planned to be away. Training became addicting. The faster I became in the water, on the bike, and on my runs, the more I wanted to push my body and mind. The body can always take more than the mind thinks. I didn't just want to finish the race; I wanted to dominate every aspect of the race and to do that, I had to learn to suffer and push my mind and body mind to accept this.

Debbie was always there to walk Gus, but in the end, he was my responsibility, and I couldn't ever expect her to do more favors. By the end of July, I had lost nearly 40 pounds. I was on cloud nine. I was feeling better than I had in years. My life had finally turned around. My mind and body felt as if I could take on any physical challenge.

After years of sulking and staying isolated, God had given me a wonderful gift of a dog. It was almost as if right after Gus came into my life, slowly and gradually, almost everything began to feel right. Before Gus, I had been falling apart, not savoring life. I had forgotten how good it could be to feel alive.

For the longest time, I had been blaming myself for how others behaved with me. I always looked inward to find a fault. But Gus came into my life and taught me that sometimes, it's best to leave behind the people you thought were your friends because, while I did that, I was slowly finding myself. I had hopped on board to a new life with Gus. While leaving everything behind, I found myself and Gus was an integral part of that journey.

Training had been going great around this time. I never really enjoyed napping or sleeping too much. However, now, it was almost as if my body gave up and demanded to rest. I couldn't help but listen to it. I enjoyed a soundless, peaceful sleep on most nights, which was a great blessing to me. Going to sleep early meant that I could wake up earlier too. I was always one for getting up early and getting started with my day. It was something I had learned to do at a very early age, working on the farm.

Saturdays were always my bike day, heading out on my long bike rides on the open roads. As my training progressed, I would occasionally perform a brick workout of bicycling and then follow that with a run workout of a specified distance. The only thing that motivated me to push harder and finish my workout quicker was that I'd be coming home to Gus. On Sundays, right after my runs, I'd return to my boy and snuggle up to him. It was nap time, and I spent it with Gus. I honestly never liked spending time away from my dog. He was a part of me. Knowing that he anticipated my return gave me bursts of energy and excitement during my bike training.

During my long bike rides, I had to be away from him for almost five or six hours. There were many times when I wanted to stop and call it a day. However, when that thought crossed my mind, I'd think of Gus. He wouldn't want me to give up. He would want me to push forward. No matter how much lactic acid was flowing through my legs or burning my lungs were experiencing, I never stopped.

In some ways, Gus was my primary source of motivation and my adrenaline push. It didn't matter if I was away, for my boy was always on my mind. Whether I was at work, at the gym, on a run or bike ride, my mind often wandered back to what Gus would be doing. I couldn't always stay near Gus, but somehow he found a way to remain in my heart.

Any time a workout challenged me, I would think about him. He helped me get back on track and never lose my focus. The faster I would swim, run, and bike meant the quicker I could get to him. People have all sorts of motivation. Gus was mine.

17

OUR NAP TIMES were early. As a triathlete, I was almost always tired and exhausted. Gus could sense my fatigue from the other room, so he never urged me to play with him. Instead, he would just quickly snuggle up and sniff me. It was a sweet gesture and gave me all the comfort I needed. He would stare at me with his brown eyes and always reassure me that it would be okay.

Our bedtime was usually between 8:00 and 8:30 p.m. I was proud of myself. I was finally living the disciplined life that I had gotten away from in the previous few years. Gus had his rituals, too. I'd always catch him pulling the covers back with his paws, fixing the pillows in place, and then pulling off his customary spin to prepare the bed for the both of us. With him by my side, I had just one less task to do: make my bed. Gus always tried to find his sweet spot in the bed before I would hop in. It made me chuckle every time and I was all the more grateful.

There were nights when my boy would sleep on the couch. Although I was happy to have the bed all to myself, having my boy lie next to me was soothing. He was my equal in the house. He always made sure to chalk out his space on the bed. There were nights when during a glorious dream, I'd be jolted awake by an awful smell. Almost every time, it was Gus's butt straight in front of my face. I would push him and make him lie straight on the bed. However, regardless of what happened, I could never sleep without Gus by my side.

Now that there were almost no distractions, completing my goals had become hassle-free. The routine was the same every day, but following it kept me sane.

Before my alarm went off, Gus would be the one to wake me up. It was a sweet awakening, and I would always open my eyes to his beaming face. It was almost as if Gus was more worried about the training than I was. In those little moments, I knew my pal would stick by my side no matter what.

My training had become almost brutal at times. After my bike rides or runs,

I'd always make sure I replenished all the fluids I had lost. Every time I would finish off a gallon of water, I'd throw the plastic jug on the floor and watch as Gus chased it like a precious treat. My boy would toy with it and pursue it, rolling it under his paws from one room to the other.

If I wasn't too tired, I'd chase him too and try to grab the jug away. Gazing at him, with his mouth brimming with that big jug hanging from his mouth, I'd almost always laugh. I loved all of his antics. I'd often catch myself saying, "You are such a crazy, beautiful boy."

Gus always kept me on my toes, even when training was off. Every time I came back home, I'd set my mind to give him time and make a snack for him. However, it was he who was looking after me. In his company, all of my anxieties and fatigue would wash away.

He was also an essential source of hope. Whenever I had a bad training session or failed to complete my specific task on schedule, Gus immediately

popped into my head. I suffered enormously because of the physical training. However, just one thought about Gus and his love for me would bring me right back into focus and to the job at hand.

However, more than the time we spent together, it was the bitter things Gus had been through and his determination to live that would motivate me. I still remember the frail and weak state I had first seen him in at the animal shelter. When Gus's struggles and the life he lived before we met flashed through my mind, I would decide that I, too, like my dog, would continue to fight on and push myself. If Gus could do it, then as his owner, I could certainly do it too. My dog gave me all the inspiration and vigor I needed to press on through my training.

August was closing in, and by this time, my training had become even more challenging. I had managed to check off most of my goals concerning my diet, sleep schedule, and workout. My routine was effortless. I knew I was doing everything right. I hadn't gone off my eating regimen once. Another thing that truly made me proud of myself was that I hadn't taken even a single sip of alcohol. Knowing that I was nourishing my body and feeding it, the right foods boosted my self-confidence.

Now, the much-awaited race was two months away. On the calendar, it looked like a reasonably long time away, and I thought of adding some cross-training. It felt like at that moment, it had become a "now-or-never" decision. However, when we feel our best, the universe reminds us that we are not as powerful or in control as we think.

By the middle of September, my body slowly began to break down. I had noticed it over the previous few weeks. My recovery wasn't as it should be. I began to detect that my morning heart rate was much more elevated than it should have been. My sleep pattern was off. I would wake up with cramps and severe stiffness in my back. Over the previous few weeks of training, I had spent a lot of time at the doctor's office, getting trigger-point injections to soothe muscle pain and inflammation. I also began frequenting the chiropractor because my body, from my muscles to my bones, felt like it was slowly giving up on me.

I started to get weekly massages to help in the recovery process. I didn't know what was going on, but I noticed everything was slowly seeping out of my control.

My only thought and obsession was my taper month-the last four weeks before the race, where you cut back on training. I had to do everything in my power to try and avoid any further injuries. The odds of me finishing the race were not in my favor. With my physical health deteriorating, I decided to decrease my workouts' intensity for the duration of my training schedule. This way, I could still train, and my body would remain in sync and be ready for race day.

However, lady luck was not on my side this time. Other parts of my body began losing their strength and integrity. One night, when I was out for a short run, I had been jogging for a few miles at a gentle pace when suddenly I felt a sharp pain shoot through my left foot, followed by a popping sound. The next thing I knew, I was sprawled out face-first on the sidewalk. I rolled into the grass, grabbing my foot, trying to squeeze out the pain somehow and make it go away.

During my training, I had always had minor issues with my left foot. My chiropractor had given me specific exercises to help with the strengthening of my arch; however, it had only been temporary. He said that I would need to have it looked at further. He couldn't guarantee that it would help me get through my race. I took his words to heart since he had been an elite athlete in high school and college. I was doing every possible exercise and treatment to survive training and "toe the line," as they say, and start my race. I knew if I could get to the starting line, I would finish somehow, and no matter what, I had to.

Eventually, I made it home. Hearing the pop in my foot and the amount of pain that accompanied it told me that this wasn't a minor injury. I could still walk, but it was something more severe than what I had been experiencing up to that point. When I walked inside the house that night, I saw Gus sitting on the landing. The look on his face was the usual, waiting for me. Somehow, all my nervousness and worries dissolved when I saw Gus. Whatever dark cloud that was looming above my head seemed to dissipate. The pain that I couldn't stop thinking about was at bay, now that Gus was by my side.

I made it up the stairs and onto the couch, and I saw Gus following me with his eyes. The moment I dropped to the sofa, Gus leaped and landed on me. I don't know for how long, but I held him in my arms for quite some time. I caressed him and tried to find comfort. He knew something had happened.

I wanted to talk to Gus and confess to him that perhaps my training journey was coming to an end. Once I had tests done, I knew they would show more than a minor sprain or the normal wear and tear. Despite all the mental and physical challenges I had faced and conquered during my training, I wasn't ready to deal with this setback.

Over the next week or so, I had several tests done on my foot. I finally ended up back at the doctor's office to review the results. Tests would show ligament damage, stress fractures, and a dropped arch. Not the best of news but better than I had expected. I left with a walking boot on my left foot, which was better than the crutches I had been using for several days. Although a bit cumbersome to walk in, I had to find a way to get used to it since it would need to stay on for six to eight weeks.

Although I was deeply saddened that I wouldn't be running the race, for some odd reason, I didn't feel as defeated and crushed as I thought I'd feel. There was a huge positive that I had gained from all this training. Despite my hard work for the race and not being able to participate, I knew that I had learned a lot. My mental health had shot up, and I had genuinely enjoyed all my workouts.

I had begun to believe in myself in a way that I hadn't in so long. To prepare my body for the race, I always knew I had to have a healthy mind. And this was the greatest gift I had received from those months of vigorous training. I learned how much one's mind and body could withstand if you yearned for something strongly enough.

18

KNOWING THAT I wouldn't participate in the race, there was still something to look forward to—my Chicago Cubs. They were in the playoffs, and we were hopefully going to make it to the World Series. I've been a diehard Chicago Cubs fan my whole life. Growing up, even though they weren't that good, the team had always been an inspiration. Every time I would watch a game, I would imagine myself out on the field, playing baseball at Wrigley Field.

Growing up, my neighbors Ronnie and Kevin would always dress up in their Cubs uniform at the beginning of the baseball season. We would get together and play whiffle ball in the backyard. We would always say who we were, pretending to be our favorite baseball player. Since I didn't have a Cubs uniform, my parents would let me take one of my T-shirts and make my own Cubs jersey. I remember not being able to choose my favorite ballplayer from the Cubs, so I decided to take all of my T-shirts and make them all Cubs jerseys, putting the different names of the players on them.

My parents were not too pleased with this decision, so I was grounded. I spent the next two weeks unable to play outside. Being eight years old and not able to go outside and playing baseball was tough, especially when you had all these awesome Cubs shirts to wear! Much to my disappointment, this would be the closest I would get to becoming a major league baseball player.

At that time, our dog, Brutus, enjoyed chasing the whiffle ball as much as we enjoyed watching him catch it. His name was Baron Brutus Von Stuben Kendrick. We called him Brutus for short. He was a beautiful male boxer. Brutus was a former show dog that was retired from the sport. That's when the love for the boxer breed had made its way into my heart.

He was a beautiful fawn boxer with a black muzzle and as regal a stance and look as a dog could have. He taught me the meaning of the unconditional love a dog has for their human partner. I just wouldn't understand this until years later.

So, I had high hopes. After 108 years of not winning a World Series, I had a feeling that they would finally win the whole "enchilada." They would ultimately be the World Champions of the baseball world.

I still remember that incredible day when I sat at the edge of the couch. With Gus next to me, we sat there in anticipation as the baseball game started. Those ten innings were the most exhilarating baseball I had witnessed in my life—moments of incredible highs and lows. But, in the end, it happened. The Cubs won. I couldn't believe what I had just witnessed. I began hopping up and down on one foot, yelling and screaming.

Tears were flowing down my cheeks, finally celebrating after all of these years of frustration and disappointment. Gus shared my happiness. He began running around the condo, barking and jumping on the couch and off the couch. Even though he couldn't understand what was going on, he knew it was important to me, and he decided to join in the fun. I knew that I had to explain to him why I was so boisterous and happy. My lovable losers, the Chicago Cubs, had finally changed the course of history. The curse tied to their name was now gone.

Gus listened to me intently and patiently sat with me in front of the TV. We were delaying his nightly walk for something for which he had no concern. I told Gus all the feelings that struck my heart at that point. He listened to me intently, and I believe I saw him nod.

When the game was over, Gus and I went out for the final walk of the night. The one thing that gave me happiness was that I had shared this momentous victory with none other than Gus. If I wanted, I could have invited some friends to the house to enjoy the game or have gone to a bar and shared the victory with the other onlookers. But I chose Gus to be with me when the magical moment happened. Being with my boy made it all the more special, impactful, and memorable.

The holidays came and went pretty quickly without much fanfare. But the Cubs winning their first World Series was the best gift I had received for that Christmas. Now that the New Year was finally rolling in, I had my sights on finally going for the Ironman in April. I had to accept that I couldn't have run my race in November, but I always wondered why everything happened the way it did. Looking back, I over-trained. There were so many signs that I had ignored. I hadn't listened to my body.

I became addicted to the drug of power, speed, energy, and accomplishment. I became obsessed with my weight. At 6'2," I should weigh about 200 pounds. I had been shooting for 170. Lean and mean. I thought, the lighter the better right? I was only ten or so pounds away. No problem. How wrong I was.

Since I had already signed up for the April race, the only thing left to do now was to buy my airfare and hotel. I had started my training but soon realized my foot hadn't healed enough to train the way I needed to. The more I ran and bicycled, the more my foot would fight back. But that wasn't all. I had come down with shingles. This time, I decided to listen to my body. I would forego all training for the rest of the year.

The pain that accompanies shingles during and after the ailment is indescribable. If I hadn't had Gus by my side, the illness would have crushed me emotionally and physically. I had thought training for the race had given me the toughest bouts of pain my body could endure. But this pain was much, much more than I could have imagined.

19

EVER SINCE I was young, I had heard about what shingles does to your body. However, the effect it has on you and the pain it causes is something you can only understand once you experience it. Nothing that I've ever had to deal with could have prepared me for the agony and misery of shingles.

While I trained, I had had to deal with illness and suffering, which might make you think that I would have learned to accept and live with pain.

Debbie was always there for me through it all, looking after Gus and doing the chores I was unable to do. She was there to offer a helping hand without a second thought, never hesitating to extend her kindness. She would take Gus over to her house and make sure he was well fed and got his walks, which gave me ample time to rest and recover from my illness.

Gus never had any issues being around Debbie. He loved her company, and that gave me comfort. I was soon out of the main phase of the shingles, only getting a short bout of them again a few weeks later. Another setback, albeit minor, was headed my way. The year before, in November, our company had moved to a larger building. It wasn't a big move—only two miles north from where we were. Having an office building to ourselves meant that we had facilities of our own. Having bathrooms to ourselves might not seem like a big deal, but at our previous location, we had to go to the nearby paint shop to use the bathroom.

I shared my old office space with another person. The room was only six by 20 feet, making it extraordinarily cramped for two people. At the new place, having my own office meant that I could bring Gus to work whenever I wanted without fear of bothering someone else. He didn't come with me every day because our office manager would bring her dog on most days. On the days she didn't bring her dog, I would bring Gus.

Whenever Gus wasn't at my side in the office, he would be lying outside in the front foyer or our office manager's room. She always had treats for him in her office, and Gus always knew who he could rely on whenever he was looking for an afternoon snack. He'd accompany me whenever I went out to the shop to talk to the guys. I did this so he would know what I did throughout the week, and what made me have to be away from him.

Jerry, our shop foreman, and Manny, one of the lead men at the shop, developed a liking for Gus the moment they laid eyes on him. There was an instant connection among the three of them. Both men had been dog owners in the past, and Jerry had lost a Husky pup a few weeks earlier to parvo, a virus. During their breaks, they would make their way to my office to say hi to Gus and shower him with their love. I always appreciated how they took out some time in their day just to be with him and show him that they care, and I knew Gus loved the attention as well. Everyone at the office loved Gus and was always excited to see him, no matter how many times he had been to the office before.

By summer, I started to feel like something was wrong with my body. We had recently remodeled the new building. We hadn't remodeled every room or office, but the interior eventually started looking like a farm or country house. Being a steel and carpentry company meant that we could handle most of the remodeling on our own. We decorated the walls with antiques from a farm. The walls had corrugated tin halfway up the wall, and then on the ceilings. In our conference room, and many a few offices, we decided to cut trees lengthwise and make planks out of them. We kiln-dried them and put them on the walls to look like siding. It created a whole new atmosphere throughout the office. It was like working in a different place altogether.

Instead of the usual paint and picture frames that one sees in an office, we had a rustic, down-home country feel. Having lived on a farm as a kid, and being from the country, meant that I immediately loved this change and how it made me think.

About seven months into the move, and after our renovations, my vision started to blur, and headaches were an everyday occurrence. I was confused and couldn't understand what was happening to me, although I assumed I was coming down with the flu or some lousy cold that was refusing to go away. It continued for a month or so, and every time it happened, my only response was to try and ride it out and wait for the pain to pass. On the days I went home to take care of Gus at lunchtime, I would take a moment or two and lie down on the bed. Gus would immediately jump up on the bed and lie next to me. He would start licking my forehead incessantly as if I had peanut butter on my forehead. At night, when we would go to sleep, he would do the same thing.

Eventually, I decided to see a doctor. After a 30-minute consultation, the doctor thought that I might have black mold poisoning. A few tests later, we would discover that his suspicions were correct. Somehow, Gus had known something was wrong.

He even knew where it was because he was always licking the same place affected by the mold. Gus knew exactly where my pain was and knew that it was hurting me, and that's why he regularly tried to lick it away and cure my illness. I've always believed that animals, especially dogs, have unique instincts that act as gifts that we humans could never possess.

My experience made me start considering the benefits of the canine community and all that they have to offer. There's so much that they're already doing; they track down narcotics, are used as therapy for the young and old, comfort children in courtrooms while giving testimony, and so much more. If pet owners believe that a dog is nothing more than an animal that belongs on a chain sequestered in a backyard without any social development or nurturing, maybe they shouldn't own a dog.

For the next three months, I worked from home until the mold remediation was complete. The time I got to spend at home, coupled with t daily medication, made it easier for me to recover quickly and regain my health. I would finally return to the office after Labor Day, 2017.

Working from home, Gus and I spent every moment together, laughing and going about our day as a team. He would be at my side throughout my daily routine, and both of us enjoyed every moment of together. I had had a 45-minute-long commute each way to and from work. Now, I got more time to work, which meant that I was working long hours. It wasn't an issue for me because at least I was at home and was fast becoming healthy again. I also got to spend time with Gus, go outside for walks, and find new places to explore. On one of these walks, Gus found a new drinking spot.

At the park, we have public restrooms with a water spout on the outside masonry wall for a hose hook up. Whenever we were at the park, Gus would always stop and wait for me to turn it on so that he could drink some water, and it eventually became a part of our routine. Debbie would often join us on the weekend. She loved Gus, and he loved her too. They had the most beautiful relationship. I could see that being around Gus made Debbie happy, and I also knew that the only person who could ever love Gus as much as I did was Debbie.

A couple of weeks before Thanksgiving, I noticed that Gus wasn't acting like himself. He had started drinking more water than usual. Summer had passed, and I knew that this amount of water was odd for him. He wasn't his same enthusiastic self either. His movements became slower, and the amount of water he was drinking continued to increase. I knew he was getting older—he was around eight or nine years old, according to my best guess and the vet's assessment. Gus being a rescue meant that I didn't have an accurate idea of how old he was, but judging by his gorgeous silver-gray coat, I assume that my guess was pretty close. I should have no reason for concern.

Gus had been on high-quality dog food from the day I brought him home, and he always got plenty of exercise and regular checkups. I decided to schedule an appointment to have bloodwork and to make sure there were no underlying issues that could be causing this change in his behavior. All we could do was hope that the results brought good news.

I remember I had been walking with Gus, talking on the phone with Debbie the day I took Gus for his bloodwork. I told her that if Gus had valley fever, I wasn't sure if I would go forward with the treatment because of my history of having dogs with valley fever. I didn't want to go through the pain and misery again, not for my sake, but for my dog's well-being. I wanted Gus to be vibrant, energetic, and have a healthy and full life rather than a life of pain.

Debbie listened to me silently. She wasn't offering any response about how she felt about my decision, but I appreciated the space she gave me to voice my thoughts and talk about my worries and fears. She became a significant part of Gus's life, mine as well.

She was a very nonjudgmental listener, and there was no one else I could talk to about the way I was feeling about Gus; and she could relate to my situation. I often wondered whether the things I talked about with Debbie brought back memories of her dog and whether it was too much for her.

20

On November 8, 2017, my worst fear came true. Gus did have valley fever. After finding out, all I could think about were the tremors, seizures, and overall discomfort I knew he might have to endure. Valley fever has no cure. There are ways to control and manage it for a while, but eventually, it gets its way.

I immediately put Gus on the medications prescribed, although I wasn't an advocate of them. I knew that he needed them. I also put him on raw goat milk, which would help his immune system. Specialized raw meat with tripe and hard kibble also became part of his daily diet. I promised Gus that we would fight this fight together. I also decided to let Gus have a say in how long we would fight this fight. He would let me know when he had had enough, but until then, I would do everything in my power to help him push through this disease.

Gus needed to have bloodwork every eight weeks, but I decided to get it done every six weeks, just to be on the safe side. The blood draws were for checking his organs' health and making sure that everything was working correctly. I monitored Gus very carefully, keeping an eye out for even the slightest hint that the disease was progressing more rapidly and aggressively than anticipated. If there were any suspicions, we would get further tests and increase the dosage on his medication.

As the weeks went on, Gus wasn't showing any additional signs of deteriorating health. He enjoyed the new food that he was on, and everything seemed to be going smoothly. We decided to stay on the course we were on, keep the same routine that we had, and continue with the new food. We would have specific times for walks and rest. For Gus, life wasn't much different than before. We still had our daily routine of early morning walks, breakfast, belly rubs, and hugs before I left for work.

For me, life had changed completely. I knew from experience that the disease would take my boy away from me sooner than later. I knew that the drugs that he was on to control the valley fever would eventually take his life. At least, that was my opinion. For me, every day with Gus was a gift. Knowing that things would turn for the worst and that our time together was limited, I went to bed, cherishing the moments we had spent together with even more appreciation than I used to. It was difficult to accept that these moments would end soon. I also realized they could stop suddenly, as well.

Our walks through the park and running into people we know, all the little moments that became our lives, would all come to an end. Everything that Gus had come to love, soon we would no longer be doing. All I could do was hope that that day wouldn't come too fast, and that it would happen somewhere far down the line to give me as much time as possible.

21

THE REALIZATION THAT I would lose Gus one day would hit me during random parts of the day. Sometimes, I would realize on our walks that there would come a time when Gus would no longer have these walks with me. When I headed home, I'd think about how there would be a time when I wouldn't have to rush home with the worry that Gus was there alone. Whenever those thoughts arose, I tried my best to push them to the back of my head.

I decided it was better if I tried not to prophesize anything sooner than was meant to be. Feeling upset and thinking about the future was just taking away from the time I had at the moment. We continued with our walks, but occasionally, Gus would stop walking and lie down because he was sore, tired, and weak from the fever. I would sit on the ground next to him and just hold him. I told him we could get up and keep walking whenever he was ready. Sitting could be from a few minutes to half an hour, and at those times, I held him and cried. I kissed him on the head and told him that I loved him. I knew that this disease was getting the better of us. That it was winning the battle, we were struggling to fight together.

As every animal owner knows, having a pet comes with the bitterness of knowing that your time together is limited and that you're going to have to say goodbye to your beloved companion one day. We all want our pets to pass on their terms and live a long and healthy life in the time they have. We want them to die of natural causes, instead of a disease or circumstances beyond our control.

Having to come to terms with the fact that there are so many reasons why your pet will live a shorter life, and there's absolutely nothing you can do about it, is difficult.

Days went by, and with them, every walk, every hug, every car ride to the park, and every bedtime snuggle become more precious. I can't even be sure if, during our walks, it wasn't me who tried to slow down time by stopping, sitting down, and resting, in a bid to steal somehow more time to be with Gus.

On the weekends, I would grab a blanket and take Gus to lie down with me at the park. We would lie under the sun for hours, and I could see the sun reflecting off his silver-covered body. A body that only got more beautiful as he aged. The silver in his face depicted the elder statesman that he was. He was a boxer, a majestic-looking dog that looked like he belonged to the highest of ranks and deserved the highest praise from any view.

He was kind, gentle, loving, and above all, my gorgeous boy who I loved and for whom had the utmost respect. We relaxed in the grass, soaking up the sun. And in these moments, I did not want to let go of a single memory of what we had together. I could not imagine, neither did I want to, the day that I would have to say goodbye to Gus. Even thinking about it in fleeting moments was painful.

Gus was my life; he had opened my heart to more love than any human being had ever done before. I believe this was why I had not been in any significant relationship. My heart belonged to Gus, my rock star. There wasn't room to accommodate anyone else.

22

I THINK DEBBIE was fighting this battle with us. She loved Gus, and I knew that her heart was hurting for him. She had become part of our family, and in my eyes, she was as much a piece of Gus's life as I was. Gus felt the same. He had a special place in his heart for her. Knowing the effects of valley fever and what it does to a dog broke her heart. We both believed that Gus's medication would take his life more quickly than the disease itself. I don't have scientific facts to prove this, but it was my opinion.

Gus had many AKA's; Gussie, Gusmeister, Rock Star, Gus Gus, and Gussers. People at work used to call him Mr. Gus. His real name is a mystery. I would like to think that Gus fits his character perfectly.

I just hope that Gus liked his names as much as I and everyone else we knew did. He seemed to have taken to it pretty early on in our relationship. There's a natural time frame for getting used to a new name, but it took Gus only a few weeks of hearing his name to begin obeying. Perhaps his early years of being taught discipline the correct way helped me succeed.

The first few weeks on his medication were extremely nerve-wracking. My mind was in a constant state of overthinking everything. Would his body respond positively to the drugs? What if he couldn't handle the effects of the medication and his situation worsened? The last thing I wanted was to barrage him with so much medication. He was older, and it scared me to think about the implications of these drugs in his system, I knew that if this were what was needed, I would do it. I'm all for the naturopathic way of healing over the conventional way, whether for animals or humans. Still, my priority at the moment was just to see Gus getting better and us being able to get a handle on the valley fever.

The time came to take Gus for his bloodwork to check his titer levels and organ functions. After the initial valley fever diagnosis, the first round of tests showed excellent results, so we were relieved. His titers were lower, but all other bloodwork associated with this round of tests was regular.

Gus and I were now entering the holidays of 2018 with great news. We were on our way to celebrating five years together. I credited the high-quality supplements and Gus's partiality to the medication for his stable health. Walking into the New Year with such reassuring news about Gus and his health could only mean that the lifestyle changes we had made for him were working out for the better.

Whenever Gus and I visited the store where we went to get goat milk, tripe, and the other items to help his immune system, we were welcomed with open arms and smiles. The staff took photos of Gus and put them up on their Instagram and Facebook pages. There wasn't a single incident where Gus was not in the mood to have his picture taken, especially when he knew that he would get treats afterward. I think it was around this time when I also started taking more pictures of Gus. I had taken photos of him from time to time, but I soon began doing this daily.

23

GUS'S FAVORITE TOY was a stuffed squirrel. It used to belong to Debbie's dog. I think there had been times when Gus and Debbie's dog played keep-away from each other. Gus would throw it up in the air, trying to keep it away from him. Other times, he would run around the condo with the toy in his mouth while being chased. Gus had so many toys to choose from, but he always picked the squirrel.

It was now winter and I was afraid that the cold might harm Gus's body. Even if it did, he didn't seem to show it. I was always hesitant about how much to walk him and for how long because I didn't want to overdo it and tire him out. I decided if need be, I would instead do a few short treks than one long walk that might be too much for him.

Gus and I started hanging out on the balcony on the weekends to take in the weather and be in each other's company. I would bring him a big, soft comforter that he could lie on as he watched the birds, and as the morning sun warmed up his body. These winter mornings were chilly, but we genuinely enjoyed them and made the most of them. I sipped my coffee as Gus looked out at the park. If there's one thing I wish I could have given him, it was a backyard for him to run and play in because I know how much he would have enjoyed it.

Back when we were in Missouri, Gus had loved that backyard, and now he was stuck in a condo where the most he could do was stand outside on the balcony. It wasn't as though we couldn't go out for walks, which we did regularly, but there was something so endearing and heartwarming about seeing your dog run free off a leash—something that I could not let Gus do at the park.

There were individual parks that Gus and I visited where he would be able to go off-leash, but there was always a risk involved that made me anxious unlike when I could let him do this at home. Being able to let Gus play in the backyard without worry and not having to keep a constant watch brought me a sense of calm and joy that I couldn't experience in our condo.

The time was near for Gus's bloodwork again. I had been doing a relatively good job of keeping my apprehensions and worries at bay. There were so many underlying concerns about the disease taking over my boy, but I did my best to push them away. Gus had energy, his eating habits were still the same, and there were no visible signs of any neurological issues.

This time around, the tests were supposed to be for his titers, not to test his organs to determine whether they were being affected by the valley fever and the medication that he was on. However, I decided that we should get him tested for everything. I didn't want to take the chance of missing something. I wanted to know sooner rather than later if there was a development that we needed to treat. I didn't want to wait another six weeks to find out things were starting to go wrong when I had the chance to get him tested right now.

Gus's weight had always been constant. There were minor fluctuations by a couple of pounds here and there over the summer months because we weren't able to go out as much, but he was never in the overweight category. When the tests came back, all the markers were stable. I breathed a sigh of relief. Gus was hanging tough.

We would stay the course and continue with the new food, plenty of rest, moderate exercise, and an abundance of love and kisses. I kept a close eye on his sleep pattern and behavior to see if he developed a head bob or twitching. Those were a couple of signs that the disease had crossed the blood-brain barrier.

But things were going better than I expected. I shouldn't have been too surprised because I had a survivor in my presence. He was a strong boy. I knew I had to be strong for him because I think he was keeping it together for me. We understood each other, and at times, it felt like he knew me better than I knew myself. If he felt any pain or discomfort, and if this disease was beginning to take over, he wasn't letting on.

There were weekends when Gus and I would venture out, sometimes going somewhere other than for our usual walk in the park. I used to mountain bike at a place called F.I.N.S., short for Fantasy Island North Single Track. It was a 20-minute drive from home, and there were several courses you could take, depending on your skill level. I was a road cyclist, so I wasn't much of a mountain bike guy. Going in a straight line suited me better and was more comfortable than navigating the rocks, tree stumps, or the 90-degree turns that seemed to be everywhere on these courses. Gus and I would take the most straightforward course up the hill, which was less taxing for me and gave Gus time to sniff at his leisure. He loved filling his nose with all the scents of the world. He was always looking for more to explore.

There was a rule posted that you had to keep your dog on a leash throughout the course. Because there were no other dogs around, I decided to keep Gus off his lead until a situation presented itself. I was pretty sure there were no coyotes for him to chase, and I felt comfortable with him roaming around and exploring wherever he wanted. He couldn't tell me, but I knew Gus loved the freedom as well.

After our morning walks, Gus and I would treat ourselves to Starbucks. I would get my usual coffee of the day, and Gus would get his Puppuccino. It seemed that Gus always knew when we would be stopping there because he would jump up in the back seat and start pacing back and forth as we got closer to the drive-up window. The regulars recognized Gus and would say hi to him and pat him on his head whenever we went.

During our walks through the neighborhood or in and around our complex, Gus always made it a point to walk to Debbie's door and see if she would be coming outside to join us. Sometimes, he just waited so that she would come and say hi. Other times, we would be returning from our walk, and Debbie would be pulling into her drive or doing some work in her garage.

As soon as Gus would spot her, he would pick up his pace. I tried keeping up with him, but the more I tried, the faster he would run because he would always be so excited to see her.

The bond that those two had developed warmed my heart. I knew Gus could never take her dog's place, but I liked to think that Gus let her know that he was there for her whenever she needed him.

24

It had now been six months since Gus's valley fever diagnosis and things were going smoothly. The more that I let myself think that perhaps we had this disease under control, the more likely it was that I would immediately become more cautious and concerned. Somehow, no matter what the signs showed about how Gus's health was stable, I was aware that we were on borrowed time. How much time, I had no idea. Neither did I want to know. Would Gus and I have two to three more years together? Would his body be able to hold up and stay healthy enough not to cause him too much discomfort and pain?

For every month that passed, I had this feeling that our time together was nearing its end. We were having the best time of our lives and making the most of it despite the reality we faced. Every memory, every belly rub, every hug, and every playtime in the park or the condo filled my heart with love, joy, and gratitude. But at the same time, it also made me cry.

I didn't want this time with Gus to end. Not now. Not ever. I knew in my heart that we were doing everything to fight this disease, which brought comfort and reassurance to my soul. However, it was hard to push away the feelings of sadness when I let myself think about what was to come.

The summer months had arrived. The heat and constant sunshine beating down twelve hours a day provided little relief. It was natural for everyone to start showing signs of being exhausted and drained from the overwhelming heat and the sun. Gus was no different. We would pick and choose our times to go out, being careful to avoid the extreme heat and always having plenty of water on hand.

We were a couple of weeks away from Gus's sixth round of bloodwork to test for valley fever, and although Gus had started to show a bit more wear and tear than usual, I had no reason for added concern. He was almost a year older now, maybe nine or ten years old, so it made sense. He was still on the special diet of raw goat's milk, tripe two times a week, fresh game meat, and his kibble.

I couldn't help but think about Lucy, who had had valley fever as well. After her diagnosis, she had lasted almost a year. Although her circumstances were different, the disease is relentless in its determination to debilitate any part of the body. Abbey and Maggie, the other two boxers she grew up with, were from the same mother and father but one year apart. Abbey was 11 years old when she went home, and Maggie was ten.

Abbey had hip dysplasia that had become so debilitating that she could no longer squat to go to the bathroom. When she was lying down, she would be unable to get back up. Maggie had an enlarged heart and other complications that made it difficult to walk without lying down every few feet. She spent her day lying around with no energy to move and no enthusiasm to try.

I had them both put down to end their pain and suffering. Maggie was the last to go home, on February 1, 2012.

25

THE FOURTH OF July would pass without much fanfare, and we would get the tests done. Gus's titers were in the negative, which was good news. All the other signs came back within range. I won't deny that I was still concerned. It became a habit to rationalize all the situations in my mind—an attempt to feel better and overcome the worry. I told myself that I should be lucky that I have Gus. That I was not even planning on adopting another dog again, just volunteering.

I did everything that I could to minimize the thoughts of what might and what would eventually happen. We would visit the pet store and say hi to the staff. They are some of the most beautiful and kindest people that Gus and I had met. They would let Gus walk behind the counter to see what new treat would soon be hitting the shelves. Gus was always the first to test the latest products. Gus had no qualms about being the guinea pig—especially when it came to treats.

Not even a week had gone by when Gus's mood changed drastically. He started drinking more and more water and wasn't acting like the usual Gus. He would drink water and then sit and wait by the stairs, telling me that he wanted to go out. Gus had always been very good at waiting to go out. In all the years we spent together, he never went to the bathroom in the house.

Except once. That time, I blamed myself. We had just returned from his eye surgery, and I needed to go for a run to keep up with my training. I left for an hour and a half, and when I came back, he had managed to take his cone off and had left a little reminder for me next to my chair that he did not appreciate me leaving him alone after his surgery. I made sure that never happened again. I had gone upstairs to find him lying there looking guilty because he knew he had broken a rule. But I had too, so I hugged him and apologized for leaving him alone when he needed me around. That day, I had cleaned up the mess and had decided against putting the cone back on him.

Gus's need to drink water kept increasing. I was confused but more worried as to why this had happened. Sensing that Gus now needed my presence even more than usual, I decided to bring him to work with me every day. I knew the guys would be delighted to have him around, and I knew that Gus would enjoy their company. I didn't want to risk leaving my boy alone if anything were to happen. I was worried about him going into seizures or getting hurt and wanted to make sure that I was there, just in case.

Although Gus was eating fine and his other movements were okay, I wanted to take every precaution possible. His habits and patterns seemed reasonable to me and at night when we were getting ready to settle in, he would take his usual spot at the end of the couch and curl up and go to sleep until it was time for us to go to bed. I used to take pictures of him lying there looking peaceful and content in his sleep.

Sometimes, I rested my head on his hind legs and rubbed his belly or squeezed half of my body onto the couch next to him and just curled up with him. With my arms wrapped around him, I would remind him that I loved him, even though I knew he was asleep. When he wasn't on the couch, his second favorite spot was on the floor at my feet with his beloved comforter.

As the weekend came and passed, I noticed Gus wasn't showing any signs of getting better. The guys at work saw it too and asked me if something was troubling him. I told them that we didn't know what was wrong yet, but that I wanted to keep him near me until we reached an answer. Jerry and Manny from the shop continued to drop by and see Gus whenever they could.

I think one of the most beautiful and heartwarming aspects of a dog's personality is that no matter how bad they feel or hurt, the love they shower on us humans remains unconditional. Dogs never disappoint us. It's as if they care more about how they make us feel than how they feel because they find an undeniable comfort in our happiness as well.

The others at my office knew Gus was sick and showed him so much compassion and love. They were so caring toward him that sometimes it would overwhelm me. They would come in and say hi to him, take turns petting and hugging him and praising him for being a good boy. Gus always knew that the others loved having him around because they made sure he knew how much they appreciated him. In a way, I think they were also saying goodbye to him in whatever way seemed best.

Some days I would glance down to see Gus lying on his comforter under my table, fast asleep. I couldn't help but cry because the reality was finally starting to hit me, and it was excruciating. My beautiful boy was dealing with a disease that was ravaging his body, and there wasn't a single thing I could do. I felt devastated and helpless. Occasionally, I would lie with him under the table and hold him. We cuddled as I held him in my arms, and my tears would slowly soak into his lovely coat of gray.

As the week progressed, Gus's condition still wasn't improving. His eating habits worsened. I went to the pet store to get anything I could find that would make him start eating again.

It was Saturday, July 21, when I made a call to my vet. I wanted to have some more tests run. I asked them for every type of analysis that would help us figure out what to do. I scheduled Gus for Monday afternoon, July 23, and the tests would be out by Tuesday.

There are signs a dog gives you to let you know they're dying. Over those few days and weeks, I noticed when we were hanging out at home, Gus would lie down somewhere in a corner or behind the chair.

Gus had never done this before. He was grooming me for what he had already prepared himself for, and it was gut-wrenching. Gus was telling me that he was tired and that our journey together might be nearing its end. I felt like Gus had accepted what was going to happen, but I still wanted to see what the blood tests would show. Maybe he had an infection that a simple shot could alleviate.

There was nothing I wanted more than to believe this. Debbie came over later that day to chat and visit to Gus. I think she knew the situation at hand. She was always someone that Gus and I could rely on and turn to when we needed a listening ear. Her presence helped me deal with the turmoil. Her presence gave Gus an additional person to share his love with and spend time with, because he was very fond of her.

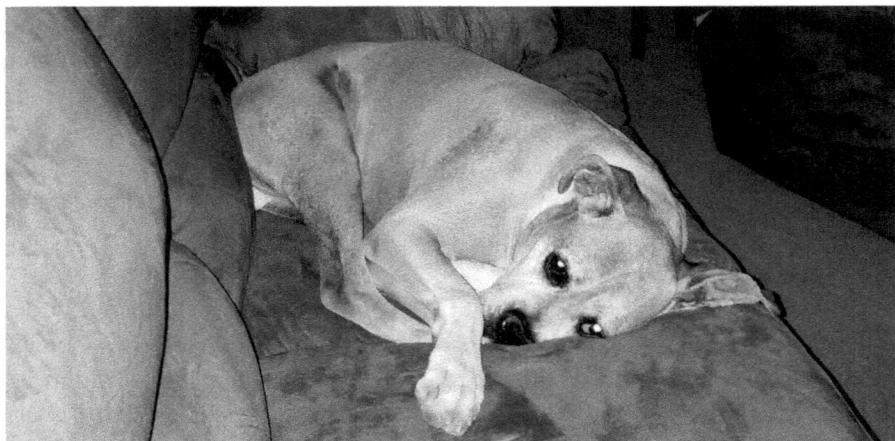

26

On our way to work that morning, I noticed that Gus had been squinting a lot. He usually sat in the front seat, but over the previous several days, he made his way into the back no matter where we were going. Gus would get comfortable lying down in back until we reached our destination. On days when he felt okay enough to join me in the front, I would ask him for a shake to let him know that I had everything under control and that he needn't worry. I would reassure him that everything was going to be okay.

In the previous couple of weeks, there had been no shakes. It had been our bond since the very start. Was this another sign from Gus? It was as if the hope I had of Gus getting better soon was disappearing with the shakes we once used to share.

I asked him to come up front that day, and he did. He was indeed squinting quite a bit. My first reaction was to immediately assume he may have developed an ulcer in his eye again. His left eye had always looked a bit different than his right ever since he had undergone a surgery to remove an ulcer he had had a couple of years before. I quickly got in touch with the eye surgeon, and luckily enough, they had an appointment available for that afternoon.

It was an hour before we had to get Gus's blood drawn, so the timing was perfect. The two of us hung out for a few hours at work as he lay by my feet as I tried to get some work done. But I couldn't concentrate on what I had to get done because there were too many thoughts running through my head.

We left shortly after lunch, of course not without Gus making his rounds through the office. By now, after months of dealing with this illness, Gus had become a different dog. His movements were slow and deliberate. His once-playful wiggle and shake were now reduced to a little sway back and forth. Although he tried to maintain his once cheerful demeanor for our sake, it was clear that this didn't come as easily for him as it once used to.

When we got in the car, I was surprised to see that Gus chose to sit in the front with me. I put my arm around him and repeated the same phrase I had now been saying for weeks. I told him that I loved him and that everything would be okay very soon. Sometimes I wondered if this was to comfort him, or something that I needed to tell myself to keep myself together.

Choking back the tears, I put my hand forward to wait for a shake. Gus stared ahead. I needed that shake from him; that gesture that was an intimate connection that represented the love we had developed, and as much as it broke me that Gus wasn't reciprocating, I knew I couldn't make him do it if he didn't want to.

Our relationship had never been about who was and wasn't the alpha. I never had to show my dominance by creating fear in my boy. We had always lived as equals, a natural give and take, depending on that trust that we had developed, where we knew that no matter if we were together or apart, nothing would ever come between us. Ever since I had brought Gus into my home, I never made him sit at the door before going out. We had developed an understanding over the years that there's a different kind of trust you build when you work together on the same level playing field.

We arrived at the eye doctor's office and were sent in right away. She remembered Gus from his surgery. She complimented him on how gracefully he had aged. She was right. His face was now an unmistakable lustrous gray, and his body was a silky grayish brown.

The doctor offered Gus a treat, but he only sniffed it and turned away. I told her about what had been going the past couple of weeks, and she just listened to me as I spoke. I had a feeling that she knew what she wanted to say but changed her mind and decided against it. She knew I was headed over to the vet's right after this appointment, so maybe she decided that it would be better to let him deliver the news. Gus had a few drops administered in his eyes, and the doctor said she would be back in ten minutes. He sprawled out in the middle of the room, and I joined him on the floor. We waited together.

When the doctor returned, I think both she and her assistant were surprised to see us lying on the floor, but they looked at us with understanding expressions. I could see it in their eyes—the concern and the sympathy for Gus and his condition. They could sense my worries regarding the battle that he was fighting. It was easy to tell that Gus had lost weight, which meant he didn't have as much energy as he used to either.

The assistant held Gus, petted and hugged him as professionally as she could without falling out of character. The doctor checked his eyes and determined no ulcers were present, but he had severely swollen eyes due to the valley fever. The conversation after that was short. I would take the prescription and begin the treatment for Gus's eyes immediately.

They offered to schedule a follow-up appointment. I told them that I would check back with them later, but even I knew that it was just a formality on their part. I appreciated them for taking the situation for what it was worth and being as patient and kind as possible.

I didn't pay much attention to anything on the drive over to the vet. I was emotionally drained and void of any meaningful thoughts except for Gus's care. All I could think about was how to help him and how we were going to get through this. It seemed impossible and hopeless, but it was all I had.

When we entered the office, Dr. Hatch, who usually isn't at the front counter, was standing there and immediately noticed that Gus wasn't his usual self. The doctor's typically upbeat and joyous voice upon seeing Gus was now gravely serious as he looked at Gus with disbelief.

The doctor couldn't believe that this was the same Gus that had been in here a few weeks ago. Once we were inside the room, Dr. Hatch mentioned that he wanted to do a CAT scan on Gus to check his brain's condition. I suggested that we start with the bloodwork first, then move forward. When he took Gus away for his bloodwork, I broke down. After trying to keep it together for so long, I felt that I had reached the end of the capacity to take in what was happening.

The doctor's face and body language told me everything I didn't want to know. Everything I dreaded showed on his face. Dr. Hatch tried to console me by talking about how well I had done in taking care of Gus over the years. He started narrating stories from when I had initially begun bringing Gus into his office and how he had grown to love Gus. When it was time for us to leave, Gus and I thanked him and left. The results would be in the following day, and he would call me to let me know.

I didn't know how to hold myself together following the visit. I was at a loss. How should I carry on? How should I act? How was I supposed to carry on with the mundane activities of daily life while knowing that my best friend, my companion, was dying, and there was nothing I can do about it?

Gus was tough. Much more than I was, in all aspects, because he still managed to pull through it all as I was falling apart.

When we got home, all I could do was sit and hold him. I tried feeding him, but he wouldn't eat anything. I offered him peanut butter, which was a favorite, but I couldn't even get a single lick.

Going to bed later that night was painful and lonely, even though I had Gus in my arms. I held him close and told him that I would be all right if he decided to go. I told him that if he wanted to go home, that I would be okay, to know that he is the greatest thing to have ever happened to me and that he would remain my beautiful boy forever. I fell asleep with him in my arms, knowing that this might be our last night together.

In the morning, Gus was still there. I helped him off the bed, and we headed off for our morning walk before leaving for work. On the way to work, Gus took his seat in the back, and I was concentrating on navigating the traffic and getting us to the office.

The vet would open up at 8:00 a.m., and I had our company meeting at 9:00 a.m. Every Tuesday, our company went through our current job list to determine their status. I was hoping to hear from the vet before the meeting started so that I wouldn't have anything preoccupying me, but they still didn't have the lab results.

Our work meetings always take place in the owner's office. There are two leather couches and a recliner that we use for sitting. Whenever Gus was present at them, he would take up a spot on the floor next to the door. I liked to think of him as our company's sergeant at arms.

My usual spot was at the end of one of the couches. Today, Gus climbed up onto the sofa and put his head in my lap. Everyone knew the circumstances and respectfully gave me a few minutes to collect myself.

Gus didn't move throughout the two hour meeting. Around 11:00 a.m., I saw I had received a call from the doctor's office. I went to my boss and

informed him that Gus's results were in, and depending on what they were, I might not be in the rest of the week. Everyone at the office and the shop were pulling for Gus and sending us their support in whatever manner they chose. He wasn't only my rock star; he was everyone's rock star.

I went into my office and made the call back to the vet's office. Dr. Hatch got on the other end of the line and told me that he had the results. He began to explain that Gus's titers were still showing up in the negative, but there were complications with his organs.

He had developed pancreatitis, and his thyroid levels were extremely high. His liver and kidneys were failing at a rapid pace. He said there was nothing that they could do for him and that everyone at the vet's office would be there for Gus and me whenever the time came. I thanked him for everything that he had done for us, for my boy, and the love and compassion that he had consistently showed us over the years.

I hung up the phone and felt my entire body going numb. I didn't want to believe what I heard. I wanted to rewind the tape of my life, erase everything that I had just listened to and start the tape over.

The night before, I had told Gus that I was ready to let go if he was ready to go, but I realized at this moment that I wasn't. I looked at my boy and said no, I need you here with me. I need to hold you, give you hugs and kisses and stay by your side. I walked over to him and looked in his eyes and told him, "I love you more than you will ever know."

It was hard to concentrate, even more so than before, now that I had heard the results. All I could think about was Gus and what we had to do next. I decided to call it a day, and Gus and I left the office. I had a decision to make: should I let the natural course of Gus's life determine when he goes home, or should I decide for him? Gus had not been eating or drinking. He wasn't getting the nourishment needed to keep pushing.

A week or so earlier, I had come across a vet who comes to your home to do the euthanasia. I knew that if I decided to have Gus put down, this was the route that I would take. I wanted him to be somewhere that he recognized, where he felt safe and could feel the positive energy of the home we had made so many loving memories in.

That night, I called Debbie and told her about the test results. I think she knew that his organs were failing and that Gus was not going to get through this. I believe Debbie wanted to tell me that it's time to put him down, but only one person could make that decision, and that had to be me. Debbie loved Gus, and it hurt her to see him this way.

We would both cry; we knew that. We would cry, knowing that all the walks would end. The sunbathing would be no more; there would be no more looking at that beautiful pink spot above his lip or the shine of the gray that now covered his face.

That night, Gus and I lay on the floor in complete silence. We snuggled as we always did. I would pull Gus close to my chest, his head beneath my chin, with my arm resting across his shoulder.

27

I HAD KNOWN since November 11, 2017, that Gus was going to die from valley fever. On the day of the diagnosis, I knew our time together would be shorter than we had planned. I just wished that the valley fever wouldn't progress, that it would stay under control. Since that day, I had repeatedly asked myself this question without a clue how to answer it: "How do you prepare yourself to say goodbye to someone that is dying?"

I kept playing over and over in my mind all the memories of our time together. I was the lucky one in the relationship. Gus had been a blessing from the start. The more I thought about the memories, the more I wanted to let nature take its course. I wanted as much time with Gus as I could get.

I didn't know what to do. I got up to lie in front of Gus to look into his eyes. I put his paw on my shoulder and rested my hand on his face, caressing him. I kissed him on his nose. I couldn't hold back the tears. Those beautiful brown eyes told me what he wanted. I went to bed that night, having decided to put Gus down.

We got to work the next day, and Gus took his usual spot on the floor beneath my plan table. Everybody from the office came in to check on him to see how he was doing. I think everyone knew that today would be the last time they would see him. Once everyone had their visit with Gus, it was time to call the vet. I explained to her the circumstances. She made a few comments about the test results I had previously sent to her, and the prognosis was what I had already known.

She asked if I knew what day and time I would like. I tried to speak, but I couldn't. The realization of putting Gus down hit me like a punch in the gut. I started crying, and as much as I tried to speak, I couldn't. She softly asked, "Would this afternoon at 2:00 work or would tomorrow, Thursday, at 9:30 be better?" Through the tears, I told her Thursday so that I could spend a bit more time with Gus. I packed our belongings and called it a day.

I told everyone at the office that I would be taking the rest of the week off. The amount of love they showered on Gus and me made me proud to know that he was my boy. In less than 24 hours, my beautiful boy would be in heaven.

Before leaving, I called Jerry and Manny. They were the closest to Gus, asking them if they wanted to say their final goodbye. They met me out in the parking lot, and both hugged Gus and told him they loved him.

On the way home, I lost track of how often I wanted to make another phone call to the vet and cancel the appointment. But I knew in my heart that what I was doing was the right thing, and it was the only thought that was keeping me together. I wanted to stop at the park for a walk before getting to the house, but the hot July weather wouldn't allow it. I wasn't sure if Gus had the energy, but I knew I didn't.

Living in Arizona, I guess one thing you have to be willing to accept is that there could come a time when your cat or dog catches valley fever. I started to wonder if staying in Missouri would have been better. Maybe things would have been okay because there would be no valley fever, and I would still have my boy.

I called Debbie to let her know that Gus was going home on Thursday morning around 9:30. I asked her if she would like to be there to say goodbye, and she told me that she wanted to say goodbye to him in her way. She came over that night to visit Gus for the last time.

When it was time for bed, I pulled the covers back before helping Gus to bed. I asked if he wanted a belly rub, and in typical Gus fashion, he turned over on his back. Gus never turned down a belly rub. We looked into each other's eyes as I rubbed his belly, and I knew that I had done the right thing. He looked at me as if to tell me that it was okay. He was telling me he was ready. Gus had fought as hard as possible for as long as he could. I let him find his sweet spot on the bed, and we embraced. I whispered in his ear, letting him know, "We will always be cuddled together forever. I love you, my beautiful boy."

Morning came too soon. The mornings were usually comprised of Gus waking up first and putting his paws anywhere on my body to let me know that he was awake. If this wasn't enough to wake me up and get me moving so I could get him outside, he would put both paws on me and push them against my body. I always responded by asking him if I could please have a few more minutes.

If I lay there for too long, Gus would stand up and stick his nose in my face. I would peek out of one eye to look at him, and as soon as I did that, I couldn't help but laugh. He always had such a look on his face that would make anyone smile. It was a look that said, "Hey, I think it's time for you to get up and let me outside to go to the bathroom. It's been a long night, and I know you don't want me going inside the house now, do you?" I would jump out of bed, get dressed, and Gus would always meet me at the top of the stairs. He would lead the way downstairs to go outside.

Today, I would take the lead. I held on to my boy and made sure that he made it down the stairs. I guess after all these years with him taking the lead, it was my turn, on this final day.

We headed off to his favorite park. It was only a few miles away, and Gus would be in the back, lying down and relaxing until we arrived. I wanted him to sit up front with me so that I could put my arm around him and shake paws like we used to, but I guess he was too tired.

We had the whole park to ourselves, so we walked a bit and then stopped as I reminisced about the time we spent together.

The park often held soccer, softball, and baseball games for the little kids. Gus would always chase the soccer ball, wanting to be part of the game. We would stand behind the bleachers, taking in a softball or baseball game, and on most occasions, the little kids watching with us would come over and say hi, asking if they could pet Gus. Gus loved the attention. His stub tail and butt would wag furiously until the petting stopped. He often snuck in a couple of kisses too. The kids would giggle and say," He kissed me," while running back to their parents. Gus loved being around kids. People in general.

We began our walk back toward the car. It would be our last car ride—no more Gus riding shotgun and making sure that I was driving the speed limit. Again, I wanted Gus to sit up front one more time, for the last time, so I could put my arm around him as I always did, rub his leg or belly as we drove, or get one final paw shake. But Gus had again settled in the back of the car and was resting.

As we turned down the last street, heading toward the condo, Gus made his way to the front seat and sat down. I put my arm around him and rubbed the top of his head. At that moment, he raised his paw, and we shook for the last time. It was as though he was thanking me for never leaving him, seeing him as the beautiful and loving dog that he was, not the dog that I had seen at the shelter. Gus was telling me, "Thank you for giving me the life I went searching for five-and-a-half years ago, but most of all, thank you for loving me unconditionally just as I have loved you."

Instead of pulling into the garage, I stopped across the street, taking a final walk around the park, where we had spent most of our time when we were outside. We walked by his favorite watering hole and then headed home. Before I could collect my thoughts, my phone rang. It was the vet telling me she was on her way. She would be there in twenty minutes. The clock was ticking way too fast.

I wanted more time. Gus had gone off to the corner of the room, behind the chair to rest. Not his usual place to lie down over the years, but recently it had become his spot.

I grabbed his favorite comforter from the balcony and folded it in half, placing it in the middle of the floor. I found a few of his favorite toys and put them on the blanket: his squirrel, the worm, and his binky.

The squirrel over the years had lost his tail and an ear. Still, it was Gus's favorite toy. The worm was a soft, stretchy toy. Gus would come to me with it in his mouth and place his head on my lap. His sign of telling me he wanted to play. I would get on my knees and grab the other end with my mouth, and we would play tug of war. The first one to let go of the worm would get smacked in the face.

The binky was a pink rubber ball with a loop on the other end, almost like a cartoon-sized ring. Gus would push the toy around the room, picking it up and tossing it in the air in front of him only to chase it down again and do the same thing all over. He would pick it up by the ring and turn to me with this look on his face as if he were asking me, "Hey, you want in on some of this fun?"

As the vet and her assistant walked up the steps, I began to cry. The vet looked at Gus and remarked that he looked tired and weak. He didn't move an inch when they came up the stairs. They said all the right things to try and

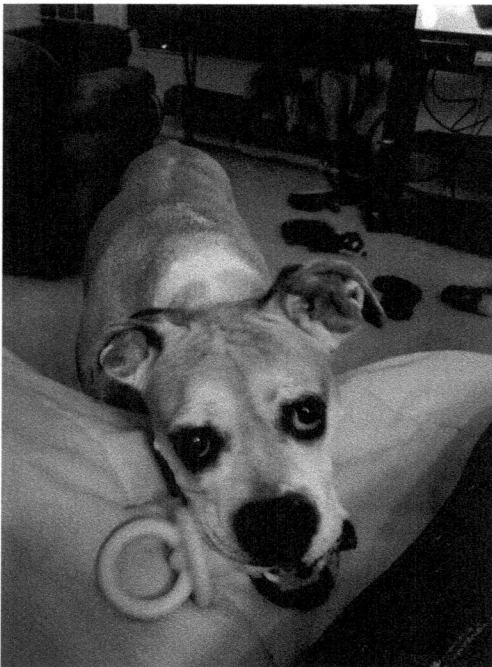

comfort me. I appreciated their efforts, but my boy was going home, and there wasn't much anyone could say to console me.

I signed the paperwork, and Gus and I cuddled together on the floor for the final time. I put one arm under his head, the other over his shoulder, with my mouth close to his ear. I told them I needed a few minutes, and would let them know when I was ready. Finally, I told her it was time and that she could go ahead and start the first shot.

28

WHEN SHE GAVE Gus the first shot, I began rubbing Gus's front legs, paws, and caressing his belly. I kept telling him I loved him. I thanked him for giving me the best years of my life. I felt Gus's heartbeat slow, his breathing getting shorter and shorter with every second that passed. Gus was in a relaxed state by now. She told me the second injection would soon follow. At that point, I hugged my boy, and I told him, "You are my rock star, Gus. We will always be together. I love you, Gus. I love you, Gus. Thank you. Thank you. Thank you for allowing me to be your partner and trusting me to take care of you."

I kept rubbing his belly and kissing his head, again and again. Our hearts beating as one, I gave him a final kiss and said I loved him as I heard the words, "Gus has passed over, he is at peace."

My beautiful boy was gone. Gus was home. No more pain or suffering. The doctor told me she would give me a few minutes with Gus and then bring a gurney upstairs to carry him down to the transport vehicle. I told her not to worry, that I would carry him down myself.

We were alone now for the last time. I was motionless, in a trance, my body feeling as lifeless as Gus was now. Not even a blink of the eyes or thought entered my mind. I could have spent the rest of the day on the floor cuddled up with my boy.

I knelt in front of Gus, admiring how gracefully he had aged over the years. I bent over him, caressing his body from his head to his stubby tail, one last time. I reached over and kissed his beautiful pink spot above his lip, which never seemed to fade away.

I whispered in his ear, telling him I loved him and that he was a one-in-a-million partner and it was time to go. I picked him up and cradled him in my arms. His head was resting on my shoulder, his hind legs straddling my waist, his front legs under each arm, and my arms around his body, as we began our last walk together.

With each step down the stairs came an uncontrollable cry. I leaned against the wall to guide me down the steps. The vet and her assistant waited near their vehicle, crying and wiping away tears of their own.

As I approached, they opened the rear door. A blanket and pillow awaited Gus. I took a deep breath and laid Gus down. I reached over, gave him one final kiss, closed his eyes, and told him, "Until we meet again, I love you, Gus."

As I stood there watching them drive away, I felt a calmness begin to fill my heart. I knew Gus had gone home to where the angels play.

With tears flowing down my face, I began our familiar walk through the park and neighborhood. Only now, for the first time in years, I would be alone. I sat at the park bench, where we would always stop. I didn't want to go home. There was no reason anymore. I would look at all the pictures I had taken of him; each one would become my favorite.

29

MONDAY CAME AROUND, and it was time for me to go back to work. Sleep had become alien to me over those few days, so getting back to work on Monday was a welcome necessity. It was also my birthday. The only wish I had was to have my boy with me.

I spent most of the day looking around my office and cleaning up. I removed all of Gus's items. Part of me wanted to jump right in and get another dog to help ease the pain. Holding another dog would do that. On the other hand, I was also thinking about being able to go places and not worry about getting home right after work or leaving at lunch during the week to get home to my boy. I had freedom now. It was a good feeling, but I felt sad and guilty at the same time.

When I found out Gus had valley fever, I wanted to take him everywhere we hadn't been together. I wanted to take him camping up north, where the pine trees covered the land, to the scenery we loved and enjoyed in Missouri. I wanted to take him to Utah, where the landscape is some of the most beautiful around. I wanted to take him to the ocean to walk side by side in the sand. I can't say we never had the opportunity to venture out on these excursions, but there is more to life than increasing its speed. Slowing down to stop and smell, if not plant, some roses along the journey is sometimes more important.

It had been just over a month since Gus went home, and I finally cleaned up all of his toys, washed his blankets, and took everything to the garage. I had decided I would hold off on getting another rescue—I just didn't know how long it would be.

After I cleaned the house and put everything away, I remember going to sleep that night and telling Gus that I loved him and wanted him to know that he was and will always be my boy. I told him that I hadn't forgotten about him and that I never will. Since his passing, I have heard his presence in the condo. During the night, I could hear him walking on the kitchen floor and moving around the house.

This particular night, however, Gus would make his presence known more profoundly. During the night, I felt Gus jump on the bed and walk over my legs. As he lay next to me, every time he breathed out, I could feel the hairs on my leg move. Gus had come to visit me. I reached over and put my hand where he was and told him I loved him. Gus was with me. He always had been and now always will, just in spirit. I think he was also telling me that it was okay for me to get another dog and not to feel guilty about it.

The next morning, I mentioned to Debbie that Gus had come to visit me in the night. Throughout our many conversations, Debbie and I would talk about the afterlife, reincarnation, and dogs in general. We talked about how dogs could communicate with humans and provide a more in-depth and valuable relationship to humans if allowed.

The more Debbie and I discussed this, the more interested I became in the idea. Debbie ended up giving me the name of an animal communicator in Australia named George Wright. I went to his website, *Wild Voices Interspecies Communications,* and scheduled an appointment. My scheduled time was for Friday, September 29, at 5:00 Phoenix time. I was hoping Gus would be able to provide me with some answers on his life before we had met. I also wanted to know if he had passed peacefully and if he was all right.

Prior to the appointment, to help George connect with Gus, I had to send a picture of Gus. I sent a picture of Gus holding one of his toys in his mouth, looking at me with a funny expression. It is interesting to note that when trying to connect you with your dog's spirit, your dog will connect with you or they won't. It is their choice, and I didn't want to expect anything from Gus either. I wished I could have made contact with Gus that day, but George told me that we needed to give him time to adjust to his new realm.

The closer I got to the appointment, the more nervous and excited I became. Each time I would think about it, I would begin to cry. The thought of hearing from Gus brought up an emotion that is hard to describe. I wasn't sure if I would be able to hold it together for the duration of the call.

When the day finally arrived, and the clock ticked closer to 5:00 p.m., I became very emotional. George would be the one to call, and sure enough, the phone rang right on time. George introduced himself and told me how the process of communication would go.

He told me that he would now try to contact Gus. There was silence. The silence which seemed like minutes was just a very brief moment. George came back and told me that Gus was there. He felt an intense and clear connection. Gus said that he had been aware of the meeting. George felt a very caring aura from Gus and a fun, silly side as well. George asked me if I had any questions for Gus, so I told him I wanted to know how Gus had ended up on the street. And why he would always stare at the wall or floor as if he were in a trance.

After a long pause, George said that he saw a young girl with long, brown hair in Gus's past. Gus had been part of a family unit, and he and the little girl had grown very close. The girl had left suddenly, and Gus couldn't understand why she had gone away, leaving him behind. He had always wanted her to come back. Now that the girl was no longer there, the parents had no reason to keep him around. They had only had him for the girl's sake. So, Gus decided to leave, saying that he was happy to go once he realized that this life was no longer the life for him. George said that the staring was Gus thinking about the girl and him missing her, wondering where she had gone.

I don't know how many days Gus had been on the streets, wandering around, searching for food, water, and shelter, but this is one of the many lessons I had learned from him over the five-and-a-half years that we were together. Gus had dared to leave a place where he was no longer wanted. He went out into the world, searching for his happiness, ignoring the fear of what might be and instead focused on finding a person or family that would love him and give him everything he needed. In return, he would be their life companion, always giving more than he would ever receive.

30

GUS SAID THAT he felt a mutual connection of love and acceptance between the two of us and that he always thought that we were on the same level. George said that Gus felt the strength of the connection, which showed the intensity of the love Gus and I had for each other.

Whenever Gus needed a little boost, I would be there for him, and he would, in return, always be there to pick me up whenever I needed it. He never felt as though he were just a dog. He thought that he was equal to me. It's how I had wanted Gus to feel from the day I brought him home. I always made an effort to make this happen.

Gus mentioned that over the last couple of weeks of his life when he could feel his health declining, our bond had grown so much stronger because I was always at his side. This was important to him. George mentioned that our relationship had been incredibly strong and full of devotion; it added to what was already an intense connection between the two of us.

Gus went on to say that he missed my touch and the warmth from my body. He missed lying on the bed and cuddling together, especially on the colder nights. He said things would be all right. It was hard for me to hold back my emotions as I listened to Gus telling me about his feelings. It brought back so many memories of the beautiful life that we shared. I missed him so much and couldn't help but wish that he were still with me- but he had never left entirely. He would always be with me in spirit.

Our time was up, and I had to say goodbye to my boy. I told him that I loved him and that he would always be in my heart. It was an incredible phone call and a soul-touching connection. It brought me a sense of closure to what happened to him and answered my questions about his previous life. Most importantly, it connected me to the greatest love of my life.

It has been a little over two years since Gus passed (July 26, 2018), and I have spent part of my time volunteering at shelters across the valley. As much as things have changed, much is still the same. All of Gus's pictures are still where they were when he was here-on the walls, on my nightstand, and on the long dresser where his ashes rest. Throughout my day at work, I pull his pictures up on my computer and look at them, comforting me when I am having a bad day. Gus was my go-to, my warm blanket. He never failed at brightening my day. He was always the best part of my day.

The portrait I had painted of him is hanging on the wall across from the bedroom. I look at the picture and wonder where time has gone. It is one of the first pictures I had taken of him back in 2013. It seems like yesterday that he was here playing with his toy squirrel. I look at other images of him that I have around the house, and I reach for the only picture of us together. I took it the morning he went home. I hold it tight to my heart. I smile and cry at the same time. I give thanks to the shelter management for allowing me to bring Gus home.

When I first met Gus, and what I hadn't been aware of, was the manager had scheduled his euthanasia for the next morning. He had previously failed the food test and dog aggression test. Gus had been deemed unadoptable. The time spent talking to the manager that day was to sway his already-made decision about Gus's future.

I explained my history with boxers, that I had grown up with them my entire life. I showed him pictures of the three boxers I had previously had. After telling my story and shedding some tears, I hoped that management would agree to give him another chance. And they did.

The next day, instead of being put to sleep, the dog in Kennel G212 passed the two tests with flying colors. From that day forward, both of our lives changed.

The other picture I took of him that morning is one I have viewed every day since his passing. He is standing still, motionless, staring at the ground. It's the look he had when I first met him at the shelter and one he so frequently displayed during our time together. I always wondered what it meant. I now know.

Gus will no longer be missing his friend. Once again, he will be in her arms, to feel her gentle touch, and hear her soft voice calling his name. I look at the picture and hope that Gus has told her our story. How two lost souls searched for hope, found each other, and along their journey together created an incredible and inseparable bond. How love, laughter, and respect were abundant, how he changed one man's life forever, and how he became known as Gus, the dog from Kennel G212.

GUS - MY ROCK STAR - MY BEAUTIFUL BOY

I FELL IN LOVE WITH YOU THE MINUTE I SAW YOU. I
BELIEVE IN LOVE AT FIRST SIGHT.

I LOOK AT YOUR PICTURES, AND STARE INTO YOUR EYES,
EVEN THOUGH YOU ARE GONE, I STILL GET BUTTERFLIES.

WE WOULD WAKE UP AT THE BREAK OF DAWN, HEADING
OUT FOR OUR WALKS.

NO MATTER SUNNY OR A CLOUDY DAY, YOU WOULD
ALWAYS SHOW ME THE WAY.

MY HEART IS DRENCHED IN LAUGHTER AND PAIN.

REMEMBERING THE GREAT TIMES AND WANTING TO BE
WITH YOU AGAIN.

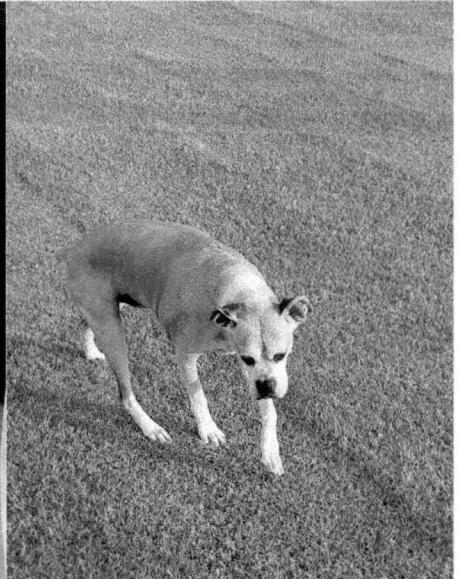

Acknowledgments

THANK YOU TO my editor and book cover design team. Thank you to everyone who supported me during this process. Thank you to everyone who showed their kindness and love towards Gus. Thank you to George Wright. Without you, my book would not have happened. Thank you to the shelter management. A special thank you to the little girl who loved and cared for Gus.

The greatest of thanks goes to my beautiful boy, my rock star, and my soulmate. A day doesn't go by that I don't think of you. I look forward to the day we will meet again and share a handshake once again. I love you Gus, always and forever.

www.ingramcontent.com/pod-product-compliance
Lightning Source LLC
Chambersburg PA
CBHW070543030426
42337CB00016B/2330